EARTH KEEPERS

Tina Ketch

EARTH KEEPERS

This book is a work of inspiration and reflection. While it draws upon myth, tradition, and science, it is intended for personal growth and spiritual exploration. It should not be considered a substitute for professional medical, legal, or psychological advice.

First Edition

ISBN: 979-8-9931385-6-5
eISBN: 979-8-9931385-7-2

TinaKetch@me.com

https://TinaKetch.com

https://www.youtube.com/@TinaKetch

DEDICATION

To the Earth, who has carried me through every season of my life, teaching me through soil and stone, river and root, that all things are alive, all things are connected, and all things are sacred. May these words be a humble offering back to the Mother who never stops giving.

To the ancestors, those whose names I carry with pride and those whose names are lost to time, yet who live still in my blood and breath. You crossed oceans, you endured trials, you carried memory through the darkness so that I might stand in the light. May this book honor the strength of your spirit and the wisdom of your path.

To the descendants, my children, my grandchildren, and the children of all nations yet to come. You are the promise of tomorrow, the laughter that heals the past, the light that makes the present worthwhile. This book is for you. May it remind you that you are not separate from the Earth, but born of her, nourished by her, and forever part of her great circle.

To the teachers, seen and unseen, human and more-than-human. To the Indigenous elders who kept alive the truth that life is sacred. To the mystics and visionaries who looked beyond the veil and spoke of what they saw. To the rivers and mountains, forests and fires, winds and stars, all who have guided me, shaped me, and reminded me of what it means to belong.

And to you, dear reader, thank you for opening these pages. You did not come here by accident. By reading these words, you step into a circle that has no beginning and no end. You become part of the great remembering. May this book walk beside you as a companion, whispering when you need courage, strengthening you when you feel small, and reminding you always that you are not alone.

This is for every hand that has tilled the soil, every heart that has carried hope, every voice that has spoken truth into silence. It is for all who have walked before, all who walk now, and all who will walk after.

With love and reverence,

- Tina Ketch

TABLE OF CONTENTS

Acknowledgements vii
Foreword ix
Preface xi
Introduction xiii
Part 1: The Twelve Steps of the Earth Keeper 1
The Call of the Earth 3
Awakening to the Web of Life 13
Listening to the Stones 23
Following the Waters 33
Walking the Sacred Sites 43
The Body as a Mirror 53
The Heartbeat of Gaia 63
Healing with the Earth 71
The Shifting Frequencies of Now 81
The Circle of Keepers 89
Becoming a Keeper 97
The Path Ahead 105
Part II Integration: Living as a Keeper 115
Seasonal Practices 117
30 Days of Living as a Keeper 121
Keeper's Blessings & Daily Prayers 123
Keeper's Action Guide 131
1. Restore the Soil, Restore Your Food 131
2. Protect the Waters, Heal Your Body 135
3. Plant Trees, Breathe Freely 139
4. Walk and Cycle More, Live Longer 141
5. Reduce Waste, Simplify Your Life 145
6. Support Renewable Energy, Lighten Your Load 153
7. Honor Animals, Free Your Spirit 157
8. Join Circles of Action, Find Your Belonging 167
Epilogue, The Keeper's Dawn 177

ACKNOWLEDGEMENTS

No book is ever born in isolation. Every page, every thought, every word is part of a greater weaving. This book, like all living things, is woven from many threads, threads of memory and guidance, of challenge and love, of grief and joy. To each being, seen and unseen, who has walked beside me on this path: I bow in reverence. I bow in gratitude. This book belongs to you as much as it does to me.

To the Earth herself, the first and eternal Mother, the great teacher, the breath beneath all breaths. To the stones that steadied my steps when I could not find balance. To the rivers that cleansed my sorrow and carried my prayers farther than I could see. To the trees whose branches offered shade, whose roots reminded me to stand firm, whose leaves whispered lessons in patience. To the winds that carried my voice into the unseen, and to the fire that burned away what was no longer needed, leaving me renewed. Your wisdom has shaped every word in these pages. Without you, there would be no story to tell.

To the ancestors, those whose names I know and those whose names have been forgotten, yet whose blood still sings in mine. You carried the flame of remembrance when the world was dark with forgetting. You spoke to me through dreams, through sudden knowing, through the quiet rhythm of my own heartbeat. This book is your voice carried forward, an echo of your devotion, a promise that the flame you tended will not go out.

To the descendants, my children, my grandchildren, and the children of all nations, who will inherit the Earth we leave behind. You are the light that urges me forward, the laughter that heals what is broken, the innocence that keeps me humble. You are not only the future, you are the mirror of all that is sacred now. May these words be a lantern to remind you: you are not separate from the Earth, you are her very breath, her song, her beloved. You are part of her unbroken circle.

To the many teachers and traditions, ancient and modern, whose wisdom flows through these pages like hidden rivers. I honor the Indigenous elders who taught the sanctity of earth and sky, the mystics who preserved the language of spirit, the shamans who walked between worlds, the scientists who revealed the mysteries of life, the storytellers who carried truth in tales, and the dreamers who refused to forget that life is sacred. I cannot name you all, but I carry your voices within my own.

And to every reader who now holds this book in their hands, thank you. By opening these pages, you enter the Circle of Keepers. You are not merely a reader; you are a participant in the great remembering. You are a co-creator of this living work. Your presence matters. Your choices matter, your love matters.

May these words serve you not only as a guide but as a companion for your journey. May they remind you that the Earth is alive and listening, that you are beloved and necessary, and that the path of connection, courage, and remembrance is always waiting beneath your feet.

With love and devotion,

- Tina Ketch

FOREWORD

There are moments in history when humanity is asked to pause, to look inward, and to remember what has been forgotten. This book arrives in such a moment.

We live in an age of both crisis and possibility. Forests burn while deserts expand, seas rise while rivers dry. At the same time, people everywhere are awakening, sensing that beneath the chaos, something ancient and eternal is stirring. The Earth is speaking. She has never stopped. The question is: are we listening?

The Path of the Earth Keepers is not a book of abstract theory, nor is it a nostalgic longing for the past. It is a living map for now. Tina Ketch reminds us that to heal the planet is not only about changing our systems, but also about changing our relationship. She calls us to remember that the Earth is not scenery, not a resource, not a backdrop; she is Mother, she is kin, she is the ground of our being.

Through twelve sacred steps, this book opens a way back into communion. Each chapter is a threshold: listening to stones, following waters, feeling Gaia's heartbeat, entering the circle of Keepers. The journey is both ancient and modern, weaving together myths of the ancestors, the findings of science, and the living practices that awaken us to a sense of belonging.

Reading these pages, you will find yourself not simply learning, but entering. You may see tears rising as you remember your first childhood moment of awe in nature. You may feel your breath deepen as you are guided into meditation with Earth. You may discover that your heart quickens as you take up the call to become a Keeper, a guardian of this planet, a voice in the eternal circle of care.

What makes this work extraordinary is that it does not isolate the sacred into temples or distant myths. It brings the sacred into your own hands, feet, and breath. It whispers that every act, drinking water, lighting a candle, planting a seed, standing beneath the stars, can be a prayer. That each season of the year, each day of your life, can be a step upon the Path.

The wisdom here is not bound to one tradition. It draws from many: the chants of monks, the prophecies of elders, the songs of rivers, the resonance of stones. In this way, it honors the great web of wisdom that belongs to all humanity. The circle of Keepers is wide, and this book invites you into it.

I believe that this book is not simply timely; it is timeless. It offers what our ancestors always knew and what our descendants will always need: a way of living that honors the Earth as sacred, and ourselves as sacred within her.

When you hold this book, you are holding more than words. You are holding a doorway. Step through it with reverence. Allow its rhythm to align with your own heartbeat. Let its stories awaken memory. Let its practices anchor you into daily reverence. And most of all, let it remind you that you are not alone. The circle is here. The fire still burns. The path is waiting.

May this book find its way into the hands of those who are ready to listen. May it awaken a generation of Keepers who will walk gently, live deeply, and love fiercely. May it guide you home.

PREFACE

This book was born from listening.

Listening to the wind moving through the trees. Listening to rivers carrying memory through stone and soil. Listening to the quiet pulse beneath my feet, steady and ancient. And listening to the ache in humanity, an ache of disconnection, of longing to belong once more to the Earth.

For decades, I have walked paths of inner healing and outer seeking. I have written about transformation, forgiveness, and the mysteries of the spirit. Yet again and again, the Earth herself called me to remember: *"You are not apart from me. You are part of me."*

The Path of the Earth Keepers is the answer to that call.

This book is not about me. It is about us. It is about you. It is about the collective remembering that is rising in our time, the memory that we are threads in a vast web, children of a living Earth, guardians of a future yet to be born.

I wrote this book as both a guide and a companion. Each step offers stories, sacred practices, meditations, and reflections to help you walk more deeply into your own connection with Gaia. But this is not a manual to be mastered, it is a path to be walked, again and again, with reverence.

You may read this book as a pilgrim, slowly and contemplatively, allowing each step to unfold in its own time. Or you may journey quickly, then return to linger where your soul feels drawn. However, you travel, know this: you are not alone. The Circle of Keepers has always been here, and now you take your place within it.

This book is my offering, a prayer, a remembrance, a vow. May it awaken in you the call you have always carried. May it help you hear the heartbeat of Gaia, feel the web of life, and know yourself as Keeper of Earth.

- Tina Ketch

INTRODUCTION

The Doorway to the Path

There are moments when the world presses in too tightly, when the hum of cities, the weight of schedules, and the restless noise of humankind drown out the quiet song within your soul. Yet beneath that noise, if you pause, if you listen, there is always something more, a whisper, a vibration, a call you cannot name but cannot ignore.

It stirs when you stand where the ocean breathes against the shore. It awakens when your palm rests upon the bark of an ancient tree. It speaks when the night sky stretches vast above you, a silence full of stars.

That whisper is not your imagination. It is the Earth herself. She has always been speaking, and now, she is calling you home.

This book is an answer to that call. It is not a manual of facts, nor a doctrine of belief. It is a path, a living, breathing journey into a relationship with Gaia, the Mother of us all. It is not a path of escape, but of return. Not a path of conquest, but of communion. Not a path to somewhere else, but a path back to what has always been.

The path of the Earth Keepers is ancient, yet it renews itself each time a soul chooses to walk it. It has been carried in the songs of shamans, in the prayers of saints, in the teachings of elders, and in the innocent wonder of children who knew the Earth as kin. It has been lived by visionaries who listened deeply, and by ordinary people who simply remembered what the world had forgotten: that the Earth is alive, sacred, and aching to be loved.

Now, it is your turn. To step into this circle. To pick up this flame. To walk as a Keeper, not alone, but alongside countless others, some living, some ancestral, some still to come.

Each step within these pages is both outer and inner, both practical and mystical. You will be invited to listen with new ears, to see with new eyes, to practice with reverence, and to dream with courage. You will walk with stone and water, with forest and fire, with ancestors behind you and descendants ahead of you. And slowly, you will come to understand that the Earth is not something outside you; it is within you. She moves in your blood, she breathes in your lungs, she beats within your heart.

This is not a journey of information; it is a journey of transformation. By the time you turn the final page, you will not only see the Earth differently, but you will see yourself differently as well. You will remember what has always been true: that you are a child of Gaia, a thread in her vast web, a Keeper of her light.

The doorway stands before you now, wide and open; step across. The path is waiting.

The Circle Closes, The Path Continues

The fire has been lit. The circle has been formed. The vow has been spoken.

You have walked the twelve steps of the Earth Keeper's path, listening, remembering, attuning, healing, vowing. Yet this is not the end. For the Earth does not ask for another book upon a shelf, she asks for living footsteps upon her soil, for hands that honor her, for voices that rise in love.

When you leave these pages, the path stretches before you into every ordinary moment of your life. Every meal becomes a chance to bless what has been given. Every breath becomes a prayer of belonging. Every word you speak becomes a seed cast into the great field of tomorrow.

You will falter, yes. You will forget. But you will also remember, and each remembrance strengthens the circle. When you feel alone, recall the unseen Keepers who walk beside you across time and distance. When you feel weary, place your hand upon the ground and let her heartbeat steady you. When you feel despair, lift your eyes to the rivers, the trees, the mountains, and know that life endures, and with it, so do you.

This path has never been about perfection. It is about presence. It is about walking with reverence, stumbling with humility, rising with love, and returning again and again to the simple truth: the Earth is alive, and you are part of her song.

You are not only walking the path, you are the path. Her rivers flow in your veins. Her mountains rise in your bones. Her fire blazes in your heart.

Carry this truth into the world. Carry it into your family, your community, your work, your dreams. Carry it as a lantern through shadow, as love through fear, as hope through despair.

For the circle is unbroken. The fire still burns. The path does not end here; it unfolds endlessly before you.

And you, beloved Keeper, are already walking it now.

PART 1: THE TWELVE STEPS OF THE EARTH KEEPER

STEP 1:

THE CALL OF THE EARTH

Invocation

Mother of stone and soil, I hear your whisper in the wind. I feel your song in the water. I know your heartbeat beneath my feet. Call me back to you. Call me home.

The Ancient Voice of the Earth

Every sacred journey begins with a call. It is the threshold moment, the tug at the edge of awareness that tells you life is more than it seems. This call rarely arrives as thunder from the heavens or as a voice booming from the sky. More often, it is subtle:

- A whisper in the wind that brushes your cheek like a forgotten memory.
- A pull in your chest when you stand before the vastness of the sea.
- An ache of belonging when you wander into the stillness of a forest.

Many dismiss these feelings as nostalgia, sentimentality, or simple longing. But for those who pause and listen, the truth becomes clear: the Earth is speaking. The call is not an invitation to visit as a guest; it is a summons to remember who you are, where you belong, and what has always been true.

The recognition of the Earth as a living being dates back to humanity's earliest origins. The earliest stories humans carried were not about empires or wars, but about the land beneath their feet. The first myths were about soil, sky, rivers, and mountains, because before anything else, people knew that life was woven from Earth's body.

Across cultures, this truth has taken many names and forms:

- **Gaia (Greek):** Born from Chaos, Gaia was the primal Mother, giving birth to sky, mountains, and sea. Her call was not symbolic; it was life itself, pulsing in every creature. To hear Gaia's voice was to listen to the essence of creation.
- **Turtle Island (Haudenosaunee):** When Sky Woman fell from the heavens, the animals gathered to help. Turtle offered his back, and Earth grew upon it. To this day, North America is called Turtle Island, a reminder that we do not stand on the Earth but with her, carried as kin.
- **Bhūmi Devi (Hindu):** Worshiped as the goddess of Earth, Bhūmi Devi is honored before seeds are planted, for her body is the soil itself. She teaches patience, endurance, and care, reminding us that the act of planting is not just agriculture but a sacred covenant.
- **Celtic Land Mothers:** In Celtic tradition, each river, hill, and valley was alive with spirit. No king could rule unless he first *"married"* the land, acknowledging that actual authority comes not from domination but from partnership with Earth.
- **Pachamama (Andes):** Mother of mountains, valleys, and harvest, Pachamama is honored through offerings of corn, coca leaves, and prayers. Her call is one of gratitude and reciprocity: she gives, and we must give in return.
- **Sedna (Inuit):** Goddess of the sea, Sedna governs the balance of life in Arctic waters. When humans honor her, she provides abundance; when disrespected, she withholds her gifts. Her call serves as a stern reminder of the importance of humility, balance, and respect.

Though the names differ, the message is always the same: the Earth calls to us not as strangers or visitors, but as children returning home.

Forgetting the Call

And yet, in the modern world, many have forgotten how to hear.

The soil is hidden under concrete. The stars are masked by neon. Our eyes linger on screens instead of skies, and our ears catch the buzz of engines rather than the songs of birds.

Life has become fast, loud, and crowded, and in this noise the subtle voice of the Earth grows harder to perceive.

Psychologists describe this disconnection as nature deficit disorder, a condition marked by anxiety, fatigue, sleeplessness, and restlessness. Children who spend less time outdoors are more prone to depression and developmental challenges. Adults who rarely experience the natural world often feel unmoored, stressed, and disconnected from a sense of meaning.

But science is now confirming what the ancients knew in their bones: we are not separate from the Earth, we are extensions of her body.

Walking barefoot on the soil, a practice now called earthing, reduces inflammation, lowers blood pressure, and balances the nervous system.

Spending time in forests can boost the immune system, lower stress hormones, and improve mental clarity.

Even looking at images of natural landscapes can calm the brain and reduce anxiety, proof that we are wired to respond to Earth's patterns.

This is the mystery and the mercy: the Earth never stops calling. Even when we forget, she remembers. Even when we turn away, she continues to reach for us, in wind and wave, in stone and star, in breath and heartbeat.

The only question is whether we will remember how to answer.

Recognizing the Call

The call of the Earth is not always dramatic. It may come as:

- The way your heart steadies when you stand by water.
- The tears that fall when you hear a bird sing.
- The sudden urge to walk barefoot.
- A longing for silence, for sky, for green.

These are not random feelings. They are memories. The Earth is reminding you: *"You belong to me. I belong to you. You are my child, my kin, my keeper."*

When you begin to notice these moments, you are already on the path to awakening. The first step on the Path of the Earth Keepers is not to know, not to do, but to listen.

Stories of the Call: The Shepherd and the Stone

There was once a young shepherd who spent his days wandering the hills with his flock. From dawn until dusk, he walked the pastures, watching the sheep graze, listening to the wind, and tending to the calls of life around him. Though the land provided for him, he often felt a loneliness in his heart, as though something essential was missing, something just beyond his reach.

One evening, after a long day beneath the sun, he lay down upon the soil to rest. The sheep huddled quietly nearby, and the air grew still. Out of instinct more than intention, he pressed his ear against the ground. At first, there was only silence. Then, faintly, so faintly, he heard it: a hum, subtle as a breath.

He held still, sure it must be a trick of his tired mind. But the sound did not fade. It grew steadier, deeper, like the rhythm of a heartbeat. The Earth was speaking.

Tears welled in the shepherd's eyes as he realized he was not alone. The land beneath him was alive, pulsing with life, carrying its own voice and song. The hum was not only in the ground, it was in him, too, in the steady beating of his chest. The shepherd and the Earth were joined, one heartbeat echoing another.

From that day forward, the shepherd was changed. He could no longer walk the fields as he once had, lost in his thoughts. Each step became a greeting. Each patch of soil, each stone, each blade of grass was kin. He began to bow his head when the morning sun rose over the hills, whispering thanks to the Earth for another day. At night, before sleep, he would press his hand to the ground in remembrance of her song.

His flock flourished, not because he ruled them with power, but because he learned to walk gently, guided by the land itself. Villagers began to notice the peace that surrounded him, the way his eyes held both tenderness and strength. When they asked what had changed, the shepherd would simply smile and say:

"The Earth has a heartbeat. I only had to listen."

And so, the story of the shepherd spread, how a simple boy found wisdom not in books or temples, but in the hum of the soil beneath his feet. For those who heard and believed, the world was never silent again.

A Modern Awakening

There was once a woman whose life, from the outside, appeared to be a success. She had built a career admired by many, marked by long hours, constant motion, and endless responsibility. But inside, she was withering. Her days blurred together in exhaustion. Her nights brought no rest, only lists of things undone. She had no energy for her body, no tenderness for her heart, no time for her soul.

One morning, she could go no further. Her body refused, her spirit collapsed, and she fell into stillness. She thought, at first, that she needed rescuing, perhaps a healer, a retreat, some therapy that would fix what had broken. But instead of searching outward, she chose something radically simple: she stayed home.

Every morning, she rose before the world demanded her attention and sat on her porch. She faced east and watched the horizon slowly catch fire as the rising sun lit it. At first, she felt nothing. Her body ached. Her mind churned. She wondered if she was wasting time.

But day after day, she returned. She breathed as the sky lightened. She watched shadows retreat and heard the first stirrings of birdsong. Slowly, so slowly, her chest loosened. Her breathing deepened. Her heart softened. The silence that had once felt unbearable began to cradle her.

Weeks passed. She began to notice the details she had never seen before: the way dew glistened like jewels in the grass, the rhythm of cicadas greeting the heat, the cool hush before the sun crested the trees. She began to notice her own rhythms, too: when her body longed for rest, when her heart opened, when tears arrived unbidden but cleansing.

And something shifted. Without effort, without planning, her body began to heal. The migraines that once plagued her lifted. Her sleep deepened. She laughed more easily. And in her heart, a quiet truth grew: she was not broken, but simply being called back.

Later, when friends asked what had changed, she did not mention therapies, programs, or cures. She only smiled and said:

"It wasn't therapy that saved me. It was the sky. It was the Earth calling me back to myself."

From that day forward, she carried a new rhythm into her life. The sunrise became her teacher. The Earth became her healer. And she knew, with a certainty deeper than words, that when all else fails, the living world is always waiting to welcome us home.

Guided Meditation – Listening to the Call

This practice can be done indoors or outdoors, although it is enhanced by being done outdoors.

1. Sit quietly on the ground, barefoot if possible.
2. Close your eyes and place your hands on your heart.
3. Inhale deeply, feeling the air as a gift.
4. Exhale slowly, letting your breath return to the Earth.
5. Imagine roots extending from your body into the soil, growing deeper with each breath.
6. Whisper softly: *"Mother, I am listening."*
7. Stay in silence. Notice sensations, tingling, warmth, images, or memories. Do not judge them. Simply receive.
8. When ready, place your hand on the Earth and say: *"Thank you. I hear you. I remember."*

Take notes afterward. Over time, you may notice patterns, symbols, feelings, or words that are uniquely yours.

Practices for Step 1

- **Barefoot Listening:** Remove your shoes and stand on soil, grass, or sand for 10 minutes daily. Whisper: *"I am listening."*
- **Dawn or Dusk Vigil:** Sit in silence outdoors as the light shifts. Ask: *"What is the Earth saying today?"*
- **Gratitude Offering:** Before eating, pause. Hold your food in your hands and whisper thanks to the soil, rain, sun, and hands that brought it to you.
- **Creating a Call Stone:** Find a small stone. Hold it in meditation and whisper: *"May I never forget to listen."* Keep it as a reminder.

Journaling Pages

Take several pages to reflect on these questions, leaving room for writing, drawing, or prayer:

- Recall a childhood moment when you felt closest to the Earth. What happened?
- What parts of your life make it difficult to hear the Earth's voice?
- If the Earth could speak directly to you today, what would she say? Write her words as a letter.
- Write your own reply to the Earth. What do you wish to say back?

Poetic Closing

The call is not thunder. The call is not a command.

It does not arrive with banners waving, nor with voices raised in force. It comes in quieter ways, in the hush of morning mist as it clings to the grass, in the secret shimmer of dew that gathers at dawn, in the pause between bird songs when the world holds its breath.

It is the sparrow at dusk, singing not to be heard, but because the song itself is prayer. It is the wind weaving through branches, carrying stories older than memory. It is the hum beneath your feet, steady and patient, whispering to you,

"I am here. I have always been here. I am yours, and you are mine. Come home."

This is the call of the Earth: not a demand, but a remembrance. Not a duty summons, but an invitation to belonging. It is the same voice that guided your ancestors, the same song that will welcome your descendants. It is the promise that no matter how far you wander, the path home is never lost.

And so you listen, not with your ears alone, but with your heart, your breath, your bones. And in that listening, you discover the truth: the Earth has been calling all along. And now, at last, you are ready to answer.

STEP 2:

AWAKENING TO THE WEB OF LIFE

Invocation

Threads of light, threads of love, woven through stars and soil, through rivers and roots, through me and through you. I awaken to the web. I remember the whole.

The Web Remembered

When you first hear the call of the Earth, you realize you are not separate. When you awaken to the web of life, you know you are not alone.

The Earth is not a puzzle made of disconnected fragments. She is a living whole, a radiant, shimmering weave of relationships in which every being, every stone, every river, every bird, every star is linked. To awaken to this truth is to see with new eyes, to feel with a wider heart, and to live with reverence for the invisible threads that bind all things.

You are not an isolated spark drifting in the dark. You are a filament in a great tapestry, luminous with connection. The breath you exhale nourishes the trees. The breath the trees release fills your lungs. The water you drink has traveled through clouds, rivers, oceans, and the veins of countless ancestors before reaching your lips. You are woven into the fabric of life, and the fabric of life is woven into you.

Myths and Sacred Traditions of the Web

From the beginning, humanity told stories not of separation but of connection. Across continents and centuries, the symbols may differ, but the vision remains the same: life is woven.

- **Lakota Sacred Hoop:** The Čhaŋgléska Wakaŋ teaches that all life forms a circle, birth, death, rebirth. Break the circle, and harmony falters. Heal the circle, and all beings heal together.
- **Indra's Net (Hindu-Buddhist):** An infinite net stretches across the cosmos, and at every intersection rests a jewel reflecting all others. Touch one, and the whole trembles. Every being is a jewel reflecting the totality of creation.
- **Yggdrasil (Norse):** The great ash tree holds the Nine Worlds in its roots and branches. Its collapse would shake the entire cosmos, reminding us that when one part falls, all trembles.
- **Spider Woman (Hopi & Navajo):** She wove the first web of creation and taught humans to weave cloth as a reflection of life's sacred pattern. Her message: *"All things are connected. What you weave, weaves you."*
- **Māori Whakapapa (New Zealand):** Whakapapa means *"to layer,"* referring to the genealogy that connects humans, plants, animals, stars, and gods. No being stands alone; every life is a thread born from countless ancestors.
- **Zulu Creation Web (Africa):** In some stories, the Great Spider wove the sky, the land, and all creatures into one fabric, teaching that nothing exists apart.

These myths are not simply poetic imagery. They are blueprints, soul maps, guides reminding us that everything exists in relationship. To remember them is to remember ourselves.

Sacred Practices Through History

The web was not just a story told around fires. It was embodied in ritual, art, and practice.

- **Medicine Wheels (North America):** Stones aligned with the stars formed circles where ceremonies and healing practices remembered cosmic order. Standing in a wheel was to stand inside the web.

- **Labyrinths (Ancient Crete & Europe):** Pilgrims walked spiraling paths inward and outward, embodying the weave of existence. Each step mirrored the threads of life's great pattern.
- **Andean Chakarunas (*"Bridge People"*):** Those chosen to live as bridges between worlds, linking humans and nature, ancestors and descendants, embodied the responsibility of being living threads.
- **Monastic Chants (Europe & Asia):** Gregorian and Vedic chants wove sound into webs of resonance. Voices became threads vibrating in harmony, aligning human souls with cosmic order.

Sacred practice was never about the individual. It was always about relationship, about harmony with the greater whole.

Science Echoes the Web

Modern science, once focused on fragments, now circles back to what the ancients always knew: all is connected.

- **Mycelium Network:** Beneath every forest floor, fungal threads weave vast underground webs linking trees into one living body. They exchange nutrients, send distress signals, and share wisdom. A single tree is not an individual; it is a strand of a forest mind.
- **Quantum Entanglement:** Particles once joined remain connected across infinite distances. Shift one, and the other responds instantly. At the most fundamental level, separation is an illusion.
- **Ecology:** Remove bees, and crops collapse. Remove plankton, and oceans falter. Remove wolves, and entire landscapes unravel. Each species is a vital thread.
- **Mirror Neurons (Neuroscience):** Your brain lights up when another smiles or weeps. You are wired to reflect the emotions of others, proving that the web is not only ecological but also emotional, spiritual, and embodied.

The web of life is not a metaphor. It is reality, sung by poets, confirmed by scientists, and remembered in your own heart.

The Spiritual Meaning

To awaken to the web of life is to release the illusion of isolation. You are not a solitary self-wandering through a lifeless universe. You are a vital thread in a radiant tapestry of being.

Every act, no matter how small, sends ripples across the web. Every kindness strengthens it. Every cruelty tears it. To live awake is to recognize that your vibration matters.

This awakening is both humbling and empowering. You are one among billions, yet you are also essential. You are small, yet the entire web reflects through you.

When you remember the web, you remember your place in the great story. When you honor the web, you honor yourself. When you live for the web, you live for all beings.

To awaken is to whisper with every breath: *"I belong. I am woven. I am part of the whole. "*

Stories of Awakening: The Weaver's Vision

There was once a weaver who spent her days at the loom. She loved the rhythm of her work, the shuttle flying back and forth, the threads tightening into patterns, the quiet music of creation. Each cloth she made carried beauty, purpose, and strength. Yet one day, as she worked, a single thread snapped.

At first, she sighed with frustration. One broken strand had caused the entire fabric to buckle, leaving gaps and weakening it. She pulled the cloth taut, trying to ignore it, but no matter how tightly she wove, the pattern was ruined.

Reluctantly, she paused her work. She found the broken thread and began to mend it carefully, stitch by stitch. As she worked, she noticed something stirring inside her, a realization she had never seen so clearly before.

"So it is with life," she thought.

Every being is a thread: every bird, every stone, every river, every child. None is unimportant. Remove even one, and the pattern weakens. Break too many, and the whole begins to unravel.

She remembered the people in her village who were often cast aside: the elderly, the poor, and the sick. She thought of the forests being cut down, the rivers running dry, the animals hunted to silence. Each one is a thread. Each one torn from the weave. No wonder the world felt thin and fragile; its tapestry was fraying.

Her hands trembled as she mended, yet hope welled within her. For she also saw that when a thread is restored, when kindness is given, when care is offered, when healing is embraced, the whole cloth strengthens. Beauty returns. The pattern lives again.

Tears filled her eyes as she leaned close to the loom. She no longer saw threads of cotton and wool, but threads of light, golden, shimmering, stretching out beyond her workshop, weaving the stars and the soil, the rivers and the roots, her own heart and the hearts of all she loved.

The weaver sat back and whispered:

"Nothing is separate. Nothing is small. Every life is a thread. When one is broken, the whole suffers. When one is mended, the whole is restored."

From that day forward, her weaving changed. No longer was it only cloth, it was prayer, remembrance, a vision of wholeness. And all who wore her garments felt something unusual in them: a quiet strength, a warmth that was more than fabric. For her weaving carried the truth she had seen, the truth that every life matters, and that the whole cannot shine unless every thread is honored.

A Modern Moment

A man sat on a crowded subway, shoulders hunched, head lowered, surrounded by strangers yet drowning in loneliness. The train rattled forward, metal against metal, its rhythm echoing the restless churn of his own thoughts. All around him, people stared into phones, clutched bags, or stared blankly at the floor. The air felt heavy, stale, filled with the unspoken silence of strangers pressed together but disconnected.

He thought to himself, I am utterly alone in this world.

Then, in the corner of his vision, he noticed a small child tugging at her mother's sleeve. The little girl burst into laughter at some secret only she understood. Her laughter rang out, bright and unguarded, piercing through the gloom of the car. The man's eyes lifted almost against his will.

Across from him, a woman sat with a book in her hands, completely absorbed. Her lips curved at some hidden line, the faintest trace of a smile escaping before she turned the page.

Nearby, an old man hummed softly under his breath, a tune without words, perhaps a memory, maybe a prayer. His voice was rough, almost fragile, yet steady, like a flame refusing to go out.

For a moment, the man's heart softened. His eyes widened, and suddenly, the subway looked different. He saw not just individuals trapped in their own small worlds, but a web of invisible threads. The child's laughter carried through the air and brushed the woman's smile. The old man's humming laid a foundation of rhythm beneath them all. The woman's turning pages stirred a breeze of possibility.

He realized that we are all breathing the same air. We are all carried by the same Earth beneath these tracks. We are all moving, together, into a shared future.

The loneliness that had weighed so heavily on him dissolved, not because his circumstances changed, but because he recognized what had always been true. He was not alone. He had never been alone.

The subway car became, in that moment, a moving temple. Each person was a thread. Each thread was necessary. And the hum of the train beneath them all was not just machinery, it was the heartbeat of the Earth, carrying them forward together.

Tears rose unexpectedly to his eyes. He looked around and whispered inwardly, Thank you. Thank you for being here. Thank you for reminding me that I belong.

And when the train stopped and the doors opened, he stepped onto the platform not as a solitary man, but as part of a living web, woven to every soul around him.

Guided Meditation – Entering the Web

1. Sit comfortably, eyes closed.
2. Place your hand on your heart and feel its rhythm.
3. Imagine a thread of light extending outward from your chest.
4. It connects to a nearby tree, then to a river, a stone, a bird.
5. More threads extend, linking you to ancestors, stars, children yet unborn.
6. See the great net glowing around you, each jewel reflecting all others.
7. Whisper: *"I am one thread among many. I shine with the whole."*
8. Rest in the light of belonging.

Practices for Step 2

- **Thread Meditation:** As you move through your day, imagine threads of light connecting you to everything you encounter.
- **Walking the Web:** Walk outdoors. With each step, whisper: *"You are part of me. I am part of you."*
- **Offering of Connection:** Each day, leave one gift, food for birds, water for a plant, a smile for a stranger.
- **Group Ceremony:** Sit in a circle with friends, holding a rope or cord. Each person speaks about what gift they bring to the web. Feel the cord vibrate as the web strengthens.

Journaling Pages

Recall a moment when you felt deeply connected to all of life. Describe it in detail.

- Draw your personal web: who and what are your threads (people, animals, landscapes, ancestors, dreams)?
- Write about one *"small"* being, a bee, a seed, a pebble, and how it reflects the whole.
- If your soul were a jewel in Indra's Net, what light would you shine?

Poetic Closing

The web is not somewhere far away. It is not hidden in distant stars, nor waiting in forests you may never walk. The web is here. It is now. It is within you, around you, woven through every breath you take.

Each inhale draws in the trees, the oceans, the clouds, the very breath of your ancestors. Each exhale becomes a gift, feeding the green world, nourishing life unseen.

Every breath is a thread. Every word you speak is a ripple moving outward, touching hearts you may never know. Every heartbeat is a drumbeat, echoing in the great circle, keeping rhythm with rivers, with winds, with the hidden songs of stone and soil.

The web is not fragile; it is eternal. Yet every thread matters. Every kindness strengthens it. Every wound weakens it. You are part of this weaving, and your choices shimmer through it.

Awaken, beloved. You were never a single strand. You are the pattern. You are the reflection. You are the resonance of countless lives meeting in this one moment.

Remember: You have always belonged. You have always been carried. You have always been seen.

Look within, the web is pulsing in your veins. Look around, the web is shimmering in every face, in every tree, in every star.

Lift your eyes, soften your heart, and walk gently. For with every step, you are weaving the world.

STEP 3:

LISTENING TO THE STONES

Invocation

Ancient ones of bone and bedrock, keepers of silence, guardians of time, I place my ear upon your skin and hear the memory of creation. Speak, stone. I am listening.

The Stones as Keepers of Memory

If the waters are the blood of the Earth, the stones are her bones. They stand where forests burn, where rivers shift, where empires rise and collapse. They have endured every season, every age, every breath of wind since the beginning.

To sit with a stone is to sit with time itself. Each pebble, boulder, or mountain is not a lifeless object, but a witness, an elder who has seen oceans form and vanish, who has felt continents drift apart and kiss again, who has held the footprints of ancestors long before your name was ever dreamed.

Stones do not shout. They do not argue. They do not hurry.

They hum. They wait. They speak to those willing to grow still enough, quiet enough, humble enough to listen.

Myths and Sacred Traditions of the Stones

The story of humanity is carved in stone. The oldest shrines, the first altars, the earliest calendars were not paper or parchment; they were stone. Civilizations fade, but stones endure, carrying the memory of humanity's prayers.

- **Standing Stones (Celtic & British Isles):** Circles like Stonehenge or Callanish aligned with the rising sun and the turning of stars. They were not only markers of time, but also thresholds into the cosmos, where people gathered to remember their place in the grand scheme of things.

- **Sacred Mountains (Worldwide):** From Mount Kailash in Tibet to Uluru in Australia and Mount Sinai in the Middle East, mountains are viewed not as scenery but as living altars, where Earth and heaven intersect.
- **Crystals (Ancient Egypt & Mesopotamia):** Quartz, lapis, carnelian, and other stones were worn not for beauty, but for protection, healing, and connection with unseen forces. They were companions in life and in burial, carried into eternity.
- **The Black Stone of Mecca (Islamic tradition):** Believed to have fallen from heaven, pilgrims touch and kiss it as a direct link to divine presence, a reminder that heaven once touched Earth.
- **Aboriginal Dreamtime (Australia):** Stories say that the ancestors themselves became stone, mountain, and river. To look at the land was to see the eternal body of the ancestors living still.
- **Native American Medicine Stones:** Carried in pouches and prayed with, these stones were considered *"grandfathers"* and *"grandmothers,"* elders whose wisdom outlasted all human generations.

From circle to mountain, from crystal to fossil, from the first temples to the heart of prayer, stones remind us: they are not dead matter. They are alive with memory, with spirit, with presence.

Science Echoes the Stones

Where myth speaks in symbols, science speaks in facts, yet both point to the same truth: stones are keepers of memory.

- **Geologic Time:** Rocks carry the autobiography of the Earth. Within them are pages of volcanoes, seas, glaciers, and meteor strikes, billions of years stored silently beneath your feet.

- **Crystalline Structure:** Quartz and other crystals vibrate at stable frequencies. This is why quartz powers watches, radios, and computers. Stones literally carry vibration, keeping time, anchoring energy.
- **Fossils in Stone:** Within stone, entire worlds remain preserved, shells of ancient seas, leaves of vanished forests, bones of creatures long gone. Each stone is an archive of lives that still speak.
- **Piezoelectric Effect:** Certain crystals, when pressed, generate electricity. They can store and release energy, acting as both a battery and a memory, just as shamans and healers have always believed.

The more we learn, the more science bends toward what myth has always whispered: stones are not inert. They are vibrating, resonant, and alive with memory.

The Spiritual Meaning

To listen to the stones is to learn patience. They do not rush. They have no urgency. They carry the long view, where centuries pass like breaths. To sit with them is to feel your frantic worries shrink in scale, to remember that what seems vast today is but a ripple in the river of time.

The stones teach endurance. empires may fall, languages may fade, but the mountains remain. They whisper: Do not measure your life by its length, but by its depth. Do not seek permanence in forms, but in presence.

The stones teach humility. To stand beside a mountain is to know your smallness. But it is a smallness that comforts, because you are not diminished, you are placed. You are part of the incredible unfolding that the stones have held since the beginning.

And most of all, the stones teach presence. Though ancient, they live only now. A rock does not dwell on yesterday, nor dream of tomorrow. It simply is. Sit with a stone, and you too may enter the silence of being.

Remembering with the Stones

When you place your hand upon a stone, you touch more than a surface. You touch memory, endurance, presence, and patience. You feel the silent hymn of creation. And if you lean close enough, ear against its skin, you may hear it whisper:

"Be still. You are not lost. You are not forgotten. You belong to this Earth as surely as I do. Rest, and remember."

Stories of the Stones: The Mountain's Patience

A young disciple once came to his master, weary of his own restlessness. His mind leaped like a sparrow from branch to branch. His heart burned with desire for progress, for answers, for enlightenment. He bowed and said,

"Master, teach me patience. For I am tired of my own hurried soul."

The master looked at him quietly, then lifted his hand and pointed to the horizon where a great mountain rose, its peaks lost in clouds.

"Go," he said. *"Sit with the mountain. Watch it. Listen."*

So the disciple went. He sat at the mountain's base in the morning when mist still clung to the trees, and he watched. At first, he waited for some sign, for the mountain to tremble, or speak, or move. But it only stood, vast and silent.

Days passed. The disciple grew restless. *"Nothing happens,"* he muttered. *"The mountain only stands. What lesson is this?"* Still, he remained, for the master had told him to.

Weeks passed. He began to notice small things: how rivers ran down the mountain's sides, carrying life to the valley. How trees rooted themselves in their slopes, sheltering birds and animals. How storms beat against its cliffs, yet the mountain endured. How sunlight touched its face each morning, and shadow cloaked it each night, yet the hill neither hurried the dawn nor resisted the dusk.

One evening, as the sky turned crimson and gold, the disciple felt tears rise in his eyes. He whispered, *"The mountain does nothing, and yet it gives everything. It shelters forests, births rivers, withstands storms, and still, it simply stands."*

When he returned to his master, he bowed deeply.

"Master," he said, *"the mountain has spoken. It taught me that patience is not the absence of power. Patience is the strength to remain, to endure, to give without demand. In stillness, it holds the world together."*

The master smiled. *"Yes. The mountain teaches not by moving, but by being. True patience is not waiting for life to change; it is standing steady as life changes around you. Like the mountain, be still, and you will discover your strength."*

From that day forward, the disciple no longer rushed to grasp answers. When storms came to his heart, he remembered the mountain. When weariness weighed upon him, he remembered its endurance. And in time, his soul became like the mountain itself, rooted, steady, patient, and strong.

The Modern Stone Listener

After the death of her beloved partner, a woman found herself adrift in a sea of sorrow. Days felt heavy, nights even heavier. Grief was a weight she could not set down. Friends tried to comfort her, but their words fell short of reaching her heart. Therapists offered tools, but nothing seemed to get the raw ache of her loss. She longed for something steady, something that could simply hold her without trying to fix her.

One afternoon, while wandering along a riverbank, she picked up a small, smooth stone. She did not know why, only that it felt cool and solid in her palm. Without thinking, she slipped it into her pocket.

That night, when grief surged suddenly and tears blurred her vision, she reached for the stone. She clutched it tightly, pressing it into her palm until her skin bore its mark. For a moment, the world steadied. The stone did not try to take her pain away. It did not speak, nor offer advice. It simply stayed, silent, enduring, unmoving.

So she began to carry it everywhere. Each time sorrow rose like a tide, she reached for the stone. Sometimes she wept into her hand while holding it. Sometimes she only sat quietly with it, breathing. Over time, it became more than an object. It became a presence, her companion in silence, her anchor in storm.

Weeks turned into months. She began to notice subtle changes. Though her grief did not disappear, it shifted. It no longer drowned her as it once had. The stone, cold at first, seemed to grow warm in her hand, as though it had absorbed some part of her pain and given her back strength in return.

She started to speak to it in whispers. She would tell the stone about her partner, about memories, regrets, and small joys remembered. It was as though the stone was listening, holding the weight of her words in its ancient body.

One day, as she sat on her porch watching the evening sky, she held the stone and realized: it had become more than a comfort. It had become a teacher.

She thought, the stone has shown me what love is. Love is not about erasing sorrow. Love does not vanish with death. Love, like stone, endures.

Later, when asked how she had survived her grief, she smiled softly and said:

"It wasn't people or therapy that saved me. It was the stone I carried. It became my friend, my anchor. It reminded me that love, like stone, endures. "

From that time on, she began leaving small stones at the graves of others, silent gifts for those still learning to carry loss, for she had discovered that sometimes the oldest teachers are the simplest ones: a hand-sized stone, steady and silent, reminding us that what is truly loved is never lost.

Guided Meditation – Sitting with a Stone

1. Find a stone that calls to you, small or large, simple or extraordinary. Hold it in your hand or sit beside it.
2. Close your eyes. Feel its weight, its coolness, its texture.
3. Breathe slowly, imagining your heartbeat syncing with the slow rhythm of the stone.
4. Whisper: *"Grandfather Stone, Grandmother Stone, I am listening. "*
5. Rest in silence. Let impressions, images, or feelings arise. They may be subtle. Trust them.
6. When ready, thank the stone: *"I honor your presence. I honor your time. "*

Journal afterward. Often, the wisdom of the stone reveals itself later, in dreams or through insights.

Practices for Step 3

- **Stone Companion:** Choose one stone to carry with you for 30 days. Hold it daily, listening for subtle changes.
- **Stone Altar:** Create a small place in your home with stones collected respectfully. Let it anchor your space with grounding energy.
- **Conversation with a Mountain:** Visit a mountain or large rock formation. Sit quietly. Ask one question and wait in silence.

- **Stone Gift:** When you feel heavy, give your burden to a stone in prayer. Later, return gratitude by leaving an offering, water, flowers, or a song.

Journaling Pages

Describe a time when you felt the presence of a stone, mountain, or landscape.

- Write about a *"burden"* you would like to lay down on the Earth.
- What qualities of stone, patience, endurance, silence, do you need most right now?
- Imagine your soul as a crystal. What would it look like? What would it carry?

Poetic Closing

Stone of silence, stone of strength, you have stood through ages that I cannot fathom. You have seen oceans rise and mountains fall, forests bloom and burn, empires rise in pride and crumble into dust.

You have carried the weight of storms without complaint. You have held the memory of fire within your veins and the cool kiss of rain upon your skin. You have endured not for years, but for millennia, holding in your stillness the memory of stars.

Teach me, ancient one. Teach me to quiet the noise within me, to rest in patience when the world clamors for haste. Teach me the art of waiting, the wisdom of bearing, the strength of standing still.

Stone of the Earth, you remind me that life is both fragile and eternal, that though I am but a breath in time, I am also a thread in an endless weave. Like you, I can endure. Like you, I can hold. Like you, I can remember.

Teach me your patience. Teach me your stillness. Teach me how to root myself deeply, how to withstand both fire and storm. Teach me that love, like stone, is not erased by time, but carried, layer upon layer, enduring beyond the end.

For when I place my hand upon you, I feel the hum of creation still alive, the heartbeat of a world older than memory, whispering softly:

"You, too, can endure. You, too, can hold. You, too, are a keeper of love. "

STEP 4:

FOLLOWING THE WATERS

Invocation

River of memory, Ocean of dreaming, Rain of renewal, Spring of blessing.

Flow through me, wash me clean, carry me home.

The Living Waters

If the stones are the bones of the Earth, then the waters are her blood. They pulse through the veins of rivers and streams, gather in the womb of lakes and seas, rise into the heavens as clouds, and return as rain. They move endlessly, circling without beginning or end.

Where water flows, life follows. It nourishes root and seed, quenches the thirst of creatures, shapes valleys, and smooths stones. It purifies, washing away what no longer serves, and it reflects, offering back the face of the sky, the moon, and the soul.

To follow the waters is to live in harmony with the flow. Water bends around obstacles, but over time, it wears down mountains. It yields, yet it transforms. It teaches softness that endures longer than hardness, surrender that is stronger than resistance.

The waters are not only a substance. They are spirits. To walk as an Earth Keeper is to honor water as sacred, to drink reverently, to bathe prayerfully, to let its rhythm guide your own.

Myths and Sacred Traditions of the Waters

From the dawn of time, every culture has remembered that water is the beginning, the purifier, the threshold between worlds.

The Waters of Creation (Mesopotamia & Hebrew Bible): In Mesopotamian myth, Apsu (fresh water) and Tiamat (salt water) combined to give birth to the cosmos. In Genesis, the Spirit of God hovered over the primordial waters before speaking light into being.

- **The River Ganga (Hindu):** The goddess Ganga descended from the heavens to cleanse the Earth. To this day, millions bathe in her waters seeking renewal of body and spirit.
- **Chalchiuhtlicue (Aztec):** The jade-skirted goddess of rivers and lakes offered life and fertility, but when dishonored, unleashed floods to restore balance.
- **Celtic Holy Wells:** Springs dedicated to Brigid were seen as portals of healing. Offerings of ribbons, coins, and prayers were given to honor their blessing.
- **Spider Grandmother's Flood (Hopi):** When humans lost their way, the waters rose in a great flood. Guided by Spider Grandmother, survivors rebuilt in humility and harmony.
- **African Water Mothers:** From Oshun of the Yoruba to Mami Wata of West Africa, water deities embody beauty, fertility, and spiritual healing. To approach them was to approach both power and tenderness.

Every culture knew: water is sacred, water is life, water is both gift and teacher.

Sacred-Historical Practices

The memory of water runs deep in ritual. People across the world wove water into their prayers, ceremonies, and healing.

- **Ritual Bathing:** From the Ganges to the Jordan River, immersion in sacred waters symbolized purification, renewal, and rebirth.
- **Libations:** Ancient Greeks, Africans, and many others poured water onto the Earth as offerings to gods and ancestors, an act of gratitude and remembrance.

- **Rain Ceremonies:** Indigenous peoples danced, sang, and drummed to call rain, honoring water as life-bringer and partner in survival.
- **Christian Baptism:** Whether by immersion or sprinkling, baptism in water marks cleansing from the past and entry into new life.

Water was never mere survival; it was always communion, always covenant. It was the meeting place between human and divine.

Science Echoes the Waters

Science, like myth, affirms water's mystery.

- **Memory of Water (Masaru Emoto):** His experiments suggested that water crystals form differently when exposed to words of love or hate. While debated, many intuitively sense the truth: water responds to intention.
- **Hydrological Cycle:** The water you drink today may once have flowed through glaciers, rivers, clouds, or even the breath of dinosaurs. Water is ancient and eternal, a carrier of memory across time.
- **Water in the Body:** Human beings are more than 70% water. Our blood mirrors the salt balance of the seas from which life first emerged.
- **Flow and Adaptation:** In ecology, water is the great teacher of resilience. It adapts, finds pathways, nourishes all it touches, and even in stillness, like a lake, provides clarity and reflection.

Water is not inert. It is alive, responsive, and eternal. Science and spirit alike reveal it as both substance and soul.

The Spiritual Meaning

To follow the waters is to surrender to life's flow. Water does not resist, it moves, and by moving, it transforms.

Water teaches surrender. It carries you where you need to go if you trust its current.

Water teaches cleansing. It washes away what burdens, renewing body, mind, and spirit.

Water teaches reflection. A still pool reveals the sky, reminding you that clarity is found in stillness.

Water teaches humility. It gives itself freely, rain to the fields, dew to the leaf, rivers to the sea. It does not cling to form, but flows for the sake of life itself.

To follow the waters is to live in trust. To honor them is to celebrate life. And to drink deeply is to remember: you, too, are mostly water. You are part of the same ancient flow that has been moving across the Earth for billions of years.

When you listen to water, you remember who you are: not separate, but carried. Not stagnant, but flowing. Not forgotten, but part of the eternal current of life.

Stories of the Waters: The River as Teacher

A young monk once came to his teacher, restless and uncertain. His mind was full of questions, his heart full of longing. He had studied the scriptures, practiced meditation, fasted, and prayed, yet still he felt no closer to enlightenment. At last, weary of striving, he bowed deeply before his master.

"Teacher," he said, *"tell me, how may I find enlightenment?"*

The teacher looked at him kindly, then, without a word, pointed to the river that wound its way through the valley below. *"Go,"* he said, *"and watch."*

The monk obeyed. For hours, he sat upon the riverbank, waiting for wisdom to reveal itself. At first, all he noticed was movement: water rushing over stones, tumbling into minor falls, swirling into eddies, and stretching into calm pools. Days passed, then weeks, as he returned again and again, watching the same river yet seeing it anew each time.

He began to notice its patience. When rocks blocked its way, the river did not resist or rage; it simply flowed around them, shaping them slowly over time. When the land dropped, the water did not hesitate but leaped joyfully, becoming a waterfall. When the valley widened, it spread into gentle stillness, a mirror reflecting sky and cloud. And always, no matter its form, it moved onward, until at last it surrendered itself to the sea.

Sitting with the river, the monk felt something awaken in him. He whispered:

"The river does not cling. It does not strive. It yields, and yet it shapes the world. It gives itself, and yet it never runs out. It is always itself, and yet it becomes an ocean. "

He returned to his teacher and bowed once more.

"Master, " he said, *"I have watched the river. I have seen it flow around stones, fall with grace, rest in still pools, and finally merge with the sea. It has taught me more than any scripture: enlightenment is not to grasp, but to flow. Not to resist, but to adapt. Not to hoard, but to give. Not to fear the end, but to return to the Source. "*

The teacher smiled. *"Yes, "* he said. *"The river has shown you what I could not. Enlightenment is not a place you arrive. It is a way of moving, flowing, adapting, becoming, and returning. Like the river, be water, and you will find what you seek. "*

From that day on, the monk carried the river within him. When challenges arose, he remembered his patience. When sorrow fell upon him, he remembered its surrender. When joy lifted him, he remembered its song. And when he closed his eyes in meditation, he heard the river flowing, flowing, carrying him always back to the great sea of truth.

A Healing by the Stream

There was once a woman who carried grief like a stone in her chest. Her days had grown heavy with sorrow, her nights long with silence. Words felt meaningless; comfort from others slid past her like rain on glass. She did not know where to place her pain, only that she could not hold it forever.

One morning, unable to bear the weight within her, she wandered into the woods near her home. There, she came upon a small stream winding its way between the trees. Its waters were clear, tumbling gently over stones, singing softly as it went. Something in its voice drew her, and she sat down upon the bank.

She did not speak. She did not cry. She only listened.

The next day, she returned. Again, she sat in silence, watching the water flow. She noticed the way it curved gracefully around rocks, the way it sparkled where the sunlight touched it, the way it carried fallen leaves gently along. For the first time in many weeks, her breathing slowed.

Day after day, she came, carrying her sorrow like an offering. She said nothing to the stream, yet she felt that it heard her. Sometimes her tears fell into its current, joining the flow as if they belonged there. Other times, she simply sat with it in quiet companionship.

Slowly, almost without her noticing, the sharpness of her grief began to soften. Her chest still ached, but the heaviness grew lighter. The stream seemed to carry away what she could not yet bear. It did not erase her pain; it held it, just as it held the rain, the leaves, the stones, and returned it transformed.

One evening, as twilight gathered and the last light shimmered on the water, she felt something shift within her. She placed her hand in the stream and whispered, *"Thank you."*

Later, she said, *"The stream carried my tears until I could carry myself again."*

And from then on, whenever sorrow rose within her, she would return to the stream. Not to be rid of grief, but to remember she was not carrying it alone. The waters would always be there, flowing, listening, teaching her how to move, how to let go, and how to begin again.

Guided Meditation – Flowing with the Waters

1. Sit quietly near water, or imagine a river in your mind.
2. Close your eyes and listen. If there is no sound nearby, recall the sound of waves or rain.
3. Imagine water flowing through your body, entering your crown, moving down through your chest, belly, legs, and into the Earth.
4. Whisper: *"Flow through me. Wash me clean."*
5. Visualize burdens dissolving and being carried downstream.
6. Rest in the sensation of renewal.

Practices for Step 4

- **Water Blessing:** Hold a bowl of water. Speak words of love into it. Drink or pour it onto the Earth, sending vibration with it.
- **River Release:** Cast a stone into moving water, symbolizing the release of burdens. Watch them being carried away.
- **Rain Meditation:** When it rains, stand beneath it. Feel each drop as a blessing. Whisper: *"I am renewed."*
- **Water Offering:** Pour clean water onto the soil with prayer: *"May all beings be nourished. May the waters flow freely."*

Journaling Pages

Recall a memory when water renewed you, swimming, bathing, or sitting by a river. Write in detail.

- What do you need to release into the current of life?
- If your soul were a river, what obstacles would it be flowing around?
- Write a love letter to water. Thank it for the ways it has carried you.

Poetic Closing

River, carry me. Ocean, cradle me. Rain, cleanse me. Spring, bless me.

You are the song of beginnings, the breath of mornings, the tears of the Earth, the laughter of the sky.

I follow your song. I walk in your rhythm. I live in your flow.

River, remind me that obstacles are not endings, they are only shapes to move around, stones that teach me patience, curves that teach me grace.

Ocean, remind me of vastness, that I am small, yet part of everything. That my sorrow is a drop, but my love is a tide, and when I surrender, I return to the Source.

Rain reminds me of renewal, that even the driest fields bloom again. That every sorrow can soften, every wound can heal, every heart can remember joy.

Spring reminds me of blessing, the hidden well that never runs dry, the gift that flows not because I earn it, but because it is given freely, endlessly, again and again.

I follow your song. I walk in your rhythm. I live in your flow.

And when I forget, when I grow parched or weary, I will return to the waters. I will listen until I remember. I will drink until I am restored.

For I am not separate from you, I am river, I am rain, I am ocean, I am spring.

I am water, flowing, living, eternal.

STEP 5:

WALKING THE SACRED SITES

Invocation

Temples of stone, mountains of flame, springs of healing, groves of silence.

I walk with reverence. I enter with prayer. I leave with gratitude.

The Sacred Landscape

There are places in this world where the air itself feels charged, where the heart quickens for no reason, where the veil between the seen and unseen thins. These are the sacred sites, temples not built only by human hands, but by Earth herself.

To step onto such ground is not tourism. It is a pilgrimage. The soil remembers the prayers spoken there, the songs sung there, the rituals offered with devotion. A sacred site is not a monument; it is a living altar, where human reverence and planetary power converge. To walk upon such a place is to enter into communion.

Every sacred site carries its own voice: a mountain that teaches endurance, a spring that offers renewal, a circle of stones that whispers cosmic order. To walk with an open heart and quiet step is to hear what the Earth has been saying since the beginning.

Myths and Sacred Traditions of the Sites

From continent to continent, cultures recognized that certain places radiated spirit more strongly. They did not build upon them by chance; they responded to the invitation of the land itself.

- **Stonehenge (Celtic-British Isles):** Aligned with solstices, its stones track the turning of the sun and stars. Legends speak of giants or Merlin raising them, but all agree that the stones hum with power.
- **Uluru (Aboriginal Australia):** The Anangu people tell that ancestral beings dwell within the great red monolith, their stories etched into its ridges. To disrespect Uluru is to wound the Dreaming.
- **Mount Kailash (Tibet/India):** Revered by Hindus, Buddhists, Jains, and Bön, this snow-crowned peak is the axis mundi, the navel of the world. No one climbs it. Pilgrims circle it in reverence, mirroring the cosmic wheel.
- **Machu Picchu (Inca, Peru):** A city among the clouds, aligned with constellations and solstices, it was less a fortress than a cosmic observatory, with stone bridges spanning sky and Earth.
- **Holy Wells (Celtic Europe):** Springs dedicated to Brigid became places of blessing. Pilgrims tied ribbons to nearby trees, leaving prayers to flow with the waters.
- **Medicine Wheels (North America):** Vast circles of stone aligned with stars and solstices. To walk within them was to walk into the excellent order of the universe.

Across traditions, the message is the same: some places are not ordinary ground. They are thresholds, doorways, living presences that call us into a state of reverence.

Sacred-Historical Practices

Throughout history, humans approached these places not casually, but with devotion.

- **Pilgrimage:** From Santiago de Compostela in Spain to Mecca in Saudi Arabia, and to Shikoku's 88 temples in Japan, walking the path to sacred places was itself a transformative experience. Every step was prayer.

- **Offerings:** Coins tossed into wells, feathers left at cairns, candles lit in cathedrals, gifts of gratitude for the spirit of place.
- **Ritual Circling:** Pilgrims circumambulated mountains, shrines, or temples, moving with the rhythm of the cosmos, aligning themselves with greater flow.
- **Silent Retreats:** Monks and seekers withdrew to caves, deserts, and mountains, allowing the place itself to become their teacher.

Sacred sites were never empty monuments; they were living companions. They shaped those who approached them with humility.

Science Echoes the Sacred

Modern study reveals what the ancients knew intuitively: sacred sites vibrate differently.

- **Geomagnetism:** Many rest upon unusual magnetic zones where Earth's field fluctuates, altering human brainwaves and perception.
- **Ley Lines:** Ancient sites across continents align in mysterious straight paths, as if mapped along invisible currents of Earth energy.
- **Acoustics:** Temples like Newgrange in Ireland or Chavín de Huántar in Peru were engineered to amplify resonance, creating soundscapes that altered consciousness.
- **Sacred Geometry:** The ratios found in pyramids, cathedrals, and stone circles mirror natural harmonies, drawing human minds into resonance with the universal order.

The ancients were not naïve. They chose their sacred places with precision, guided by listening, intuition, and a science that was not yet fully understood.

The Spiritual Meaning

To walk sacred sites is to step into a relationship. A site is not a backdrop for your photos; it is a presence, a being, a teacher. When you walk reverently, you enter into dialogue with the land itself.

And sacredness is not limited to the famous places of the world. A grove near your home, a quiet spring, a stone that draws you, these too are sacred. What makes a site holy is not only grandeur, but awareness. Reverence transforms ordinary ground into sacred ground.

When you walk with humility, you join a lineage of devotion. Your footsteps mingle with those of countless pilgrims who came before you. Your prayers weave into a tapestry of centuries. You walk not as a tourist, but as a pilgrim.

To walk sacred sites is to remember that the Earth herself is a temple, and every step upon her is holy ground.

Stories of Pilgrimage: The Pilgrim at Glastonbury

There was once a seeker who journeyed to Glastonbury, the ancient heart of England's sacred landscape. For years, she had read of Avalon, the isle of mystery veiled in mist, a place where the old ways still breathed. Something within her longed to touch that mystery, not through books or stories, but with her own feet, her own breath, her own soul.

At dawn, she began the climb up Glastonbury Tor. The path wound steeply, the grass slick with dew. Mist swirled thick around her, curling like smoke, cloaking the hill in secrecy. Each step felt both ordinary and otherworldly, as if she were walking not only upward, but inward, into a place within herself she had long forgotten.

She climbed slowly, her heart pounding, her breath rising in clouds of vapor. The bells of the town below faded until all she could hear was the sound of her own footsteps and the whisper of wind through the mist. The Tor seemed alive, its slope humming with presence, its silence drawing her deeper into herself.

When she reached the summit, the veil of mist parted slightly, revealing the lone tower of St. Michael rising against the pale sky. She stepped closer, her hands brushing the stone, calm and rough beneath her fingertips.

And then, without warning, the world fell utterly silent. The wind stilled. The birds ceased their calls. In that stillness, something opened inside her chest, wide, vast, infinite. It was as though the Earth herself breathed through her, filling her lungs with ancient memory, filling her heart with something beyond words.

Tears rose, unbidden. She had come searching for Avalon, for a place spoken of in legend, a land of priestesses and kings, of magic and mystery. But what she found was not an external kingdom; it was the sacredness within her own being.

Later, when asked what she had discovered upon the Tor, she smiled softly through tears and said:

"I did not find Avalon. I found my own heart. I found that the isle of mist was never lost, it was waiting within me all along."

From that day forward, Glastonbury lived in her not only as a place on a map, but as a living reminder: that pilgrimage is not about reaching a destination, but about awakening to what has always been present. The Earth does not give us something we lack; it mirrors back the holiness we have forgotten.

And so, when she left the Tor, she did not feel as though she was leaving sacred ground. She carried it with her, with every breath, every step, every prayer of gratitude. For the Tor had not revealed Avalon, it had revealed herself.

The Unknown Hill

There was once a man bowed beneath the weight of grief. The loss he carried was too significant for words, too heavy for comfort. His home felt suffocating, his days empty, his nights restless. He wandered without destination, hoping that walking might somehow ease what his heart could not bear.

One gray afternoon, his feet led him into the countryside. The sky hung low, heavy with clouds, and the air smelled of rain. He walked through meadows dotted with wildflowers, past hedgerows humming with unseen birds, until at last he came to a hill rising gently from the land. It was unmarked, uncelebrated, nothing to distinguish it from the rest of the rolling fields, yet something about it drew him.

He climbed slowly, each step an effort, the weight of sorrow pressing down on his chest. But as he reached the crest and stood upon its crown, something shifted. The wind softened. The silence deepened. The hill seemed to hold him, as if the Earth itself had opened its arms.

For the first time in many weeks, he felt peace, not an end to his grief, but a stillness that cradled it. He sat down upon the grass, his hands pressed to the soil. The ground felt warm, steady, alive. He closed his eyes, and a strange calm washed over him, as though the hill was breathing with him, as though unseen voices whispered gently through the roots and stones: You are not alone. You are held.

He returned to that hill again and again. Sometimes he sat in silence. Sometimes he wept openly, letting his tears fall into the earth. Each time, he left feeling lighter, as if the hill had absorbed some of his sorrow and returned him a little more strength.

Months later, he learned from a local villager that the hill was no ordinary rise of land. It was an ancient burial mound, revered for thousands of years. Generations had come there to mourn, to pray, to honor the dead. The ground itself had been hallowed by centuries of tears and offerings, made sacred by the lives it cradled.

Hearing this, the man felt tears come again, this time not only from grief, but also from awe and gratitude.

"I thought I had stumbled upon a quiet place," he whispered, *"but it was the place that found me. The hill knew my sorrow before I ever arrived. It was waiting for me, as it has waited for countless others. I did not choose it, it chose me."*

From then on, he no longer walked with despair, but with reverence. He understood that the Earth holds us not only in life, but in loss. And he carried the lesson of the unknown hill wherever he went: that sometimes the healing we need does not come from seeking, but from being found.

Guided Meditation – Entering a Sacred Site

1. Close your eyes and imagine standing at the edge of a sacred place.
2. Place your hand on your heart. Whisper: *"I enter with reverence."*
3. Imagine walking slowly, each step a prayer.
4. Feel the ground beneath your feet, the air upon your skin, the presence surrounding you.
5. Ask silently: *"What do you wish to teach me?"*
6. Listen. Receive impressions, images, or silence. All are sacred.
7. When you leave, bow inwardly. Whisper: *"I leave with gratitude."*

Practices for Step 5

- **Approaching the Sacred:** Pause before entering any place that feels holy. Place your hand on your heart. Enter slowly, as if crossing a threshold.

- **Pilgrim's Prayer Walk:** Walk in silence through a natural or built sacred site. Match your steps to your breath.
- **Offering Ceremony:** Leave a simple gift, flower, song, or prayer, not as payment, but recognition.
- **Inner Sacred Site:** If you cannot travel, imagine a holy place in meditation. Walk its paths with your soul.

Journaling Pages

- Recall a place that felt sacred to you. What made it different?
- How do you feel when you enter temples, forests, or circles of stone?
- If you built a sacred site for future generations, what would it look like?
- What everyday places in your life could become sacred if entered with reverence?

Poetic Closing

Every stone is a temple, holding the memory of fire and time, whispering the hymns of the Earth's first breath.

Every spring is a font, flowing with renewal, carrying the blessings of clouds and sky, offering life freely to all who thirst.

Every hill is an altar, rising steady and patient, lifting prayers of soil and seed toward the heavens, a meeting ground between Earth and sky.

Every grove is a shrine, where silence becomes song, and the breath of the trees joins your own.

The sacred is not far away. It is not hidden in distant lands or locked within ancient monuments. It is here, beneath your feet, in the air you breathe, in the water that touches your lips, in the ground that cradles your steps.

To walk this Earth is to walk through a cathedral. Each step is a prayer. Each breath is a hymn. Each heartbeat joins the great liturgy of life.

Walk gently, beloved. Walk with reverence. For every place is holy ground, and every moment is an altar where you may bow, remember, and give thanks.

STEP 6:

THE BODY AS A MIRROR

Invocation

Bones of mountains, blood of rivers, breath of forests, heart of fire.

I look within, and see the Earth. I honor the mirror.

The Body of Earth

The Earth and the human body are not two; they are one.

Your skin is her soil, holding the memory of sun and rain. Your bones are her mountains, strong, enduring, carrying the weight of time. Your blood is her rivers and seas, salty with the same minerals that once filled the ancient oceans. Your breath is her wind, moving in rhythm with the forests. Your heart is her molten core, a fire that burns steadily, giving warmth and life.

When you awaken to this truth, something changes in how you walk. No longer is your body a burden to discipline, deny, or reject; it becomes a sacred temple, a reflection of the living Earth herself. Every ache becomes weather passing through you. Every heartbeat becomes a drum echoing the pulse of creation. Every breath becomes a communion.

To live in this awareness is to live as part of a great body, the body of the Earth, the body of the cosmos.

Myths and Sacred Traditions of the Cosmic Body

Cultures across time have remembered: our bodies are not separate, they are reflections of the universe itself.

- **Puruṣa (Hindu Vedas):** From the cosmic being Puruṣa, the universe was born. His mouth became the priests, his arms the warriors, his thighs the farmers, his feet the servants. The human body was not only flesh, it was society, cosmos, and divine order embodied.
- **Ymir (Norse):** From the primordial giant Ymir, slain by the gods, the world was shaped: his flesh became Earth, his bones the mountains, his blood the seas, his skull the sky. Humanity lives within the body of a giant ancestor.
- **Macrocosm and Microcosm (Hermetic Tradition):** *"As above, so below."* The human body reflects the cosmos, and the cosmos reflects the body. What lives in the stars lives also in your blood and breath.
- **Māori Breath of Life (New Zealand):** The first human inhaled the very breath of the Earth, and every breath since is a continuation of that moment. Breath unites humanity and Earth in one eternal exchange.
- **Andean Q'ero People (Peru):** Healers speak of sami, a refined energy that flows between Earth and humans, exchanged through breath and body, making each person a bridge between heaven and Earth.

These myths remind us: to know yourself is to understand Earth, and to honor Earth is to honor yourself.

Sacred-Historical Views of the Body

Not only myth, but medicine and spirituality across history have recognized the sacred reflection of Earth in the human body.

- **Ayurveda (India):** The five elements, earth, water, fire, air, and ether, are expressed in the body as doshas. Health is balance within, which mirrors balance with the Earth.
- **Chinese Medicine:** Meridians are rivers of energy, flowing through the body as rivers flow through Earth. Illness arises when flow is blocked; healing is the restoration of harmony.

- **Mystical Christianity:** *"Do you not know that your body is a temple of the Holy Spirit?"* To care for your body is to honor divine presence within creation itself.
- **Indigenous Teachings:** Many traditions teach that your body is the first land you must learn to care for. How you treat your flesh is how you treat the Earth.

The wisdom of every culture whispers the same truth: your body is not separate, it is the sacred world made visible.

Science Echoes the Mirror

Where myth and medicine sing in story, science confirms in fact.

- **Elements:** The calcium in your bones was forged in ancient stars. The iron in your blood mirrors the molten iron at Earth's core. You are literally stardust embodied.
- **Water:** The human body is ~70% water, just as Earth's surface is ~70% water. The salt in your blood mirrors the salt of the primordial seas.
- **Breath:** Every inhale carries oxygen made by trees, and every exhale returns carbon dioxide that nourishes them. Your lungs are forests in miniature.
- **Circulation:** Rivers and blood vessels mirror one another, both flowing, both carrying nutrients, both stagnant when blocked, both healed by movement.
- **Neurons and Lightning:** The branching patterns of your neurons resemble lightning, river deltas, and galaxies. Energy moves through you in the same fractal patterns that shape the universe.

Science affirms what myth has always known: you are Earth embodied.

The Spiritual Meaning

To see your body as Earth is to dissolve shame. No longer is it an enemy to conquer or a flawed object to control; it is a temple, a teacher, a holy landscape.

It is also to dissolve the separation. When you harm your body, you harm Earth. When you heal your body, you heal Earth. When you honor your body, you honor Earth. The two are not distinct, they are one.

And this awakening births compassion. You begin to care for your body as you would a sacred mountain, treating it with reverence, patience, and gratitude. You walk gently on Earth as you would within your own skin.

When you awaken to this mirror, you no longer live as a stranger in your own body, nor as a stranger on the Earth. You remember that you are woven of the same elements, carried by the same breath, alive with the same pulse.

And when you finally look within and see the Earth, you will bow, not in fear, but in love.

Stories of the Mirror: The Monk and the Mountain

There was once a young monk who had given his life to practice. He rose before dawn each day, sat upon his cushion, and sought to still his restless mind. But no matter how long he sat, thoughts flooded him like flocks of birds scattering in all directions. Memories, desires, regrets, and dreams filled his head until he grew weary and discouraged.

One morning, after a night of tossing in restless sleep, the monk went outside to meditate beneath the open sky. In front of the monastery rose a great mountain, its slopes covered in pines, its peak crowned with clouds. He sat facing it, but even there his mind would not quiet. His breath was ragged, his heart raced, and frustration boiled within him.

Finally, he cried out in despair, *"Why can't I be steady? Why can't I sit in peace?"*

The mountain gave no reply. It simply remained, vast and silent, unmoved by his outburst.

The monk glared at it through tears of weariness. Yet as he stared, something subtle began to change. He noticed the mountain's unshakable presence. Winds rushed around it, storms gathered and passed, rivers ran down its sides, yet the mountain itself did not waver. It stood as it had for centuries, rooted deep in the Earth, patient, unhurried, at rest in its own being.

A thought stirred in the monk's heart: The mountain is not trying to be steady. It simply is steady. It does not struggle to hold still, it is stillness itself.

Suddenly, he understood.

"My spine is a mountain," he whispered. *"If I sit as the mountain sits, rooted, grounded, unmoved, my mind will follow."*

So he straightened his back. He imagined his spine as the mountain's ridge, strong and unwavering. His hips were its base, rooted deeply in the Earth. His shoulders were slopes, his head the summit rising into sky. He breathed as if winds moved across his surface, yet within remained still.

Slowly, his body softened into this image. His breath slowed, his thoughts quieted. The turmoil of his mind did not vanish immediately, but it no longer tossed him about. Like clouds around a mountain peak, thoughts came and went, but the mountain remained.

From that day on, his meditation changed. He no longer sat as a man battling his mind. He sat as the mountain sits, steady, patient, enduring. When storms of thought arose, he let them come and pass. When winds of emotion blew, he did not resist. He simply sat, as mountain, as stillness.

Years later, when asked about the secret of his deep peace, the monk smiled and pointed toward the mountain.

"The mountain taught me," he said. *"It showed me that steadiness is not something I must force. It is something I already am. When I remember my spine is a mountain, my heart becomes the sky."*

The Healer and the River

There was once a healer who lived in a small village surrounded by forests and streams. People came to her not only for herbs and remedies, but for wisdom. She listened with patience, and often her prescriptions were not only tinctures or teas, but stories, prayers, and invitations to listen to the Earth.

One day, a patient came to her weary and pale. His body felt heavy, his blood sluggish, his spirit dull. *"I feel as though life no longer moves through me,"* he confessed.

The healer nodded gently, and instead of reaching for her jars or grinding roots, she said, *"Come with me."* She led him down a winding path until they reached the river that flowed at the edge of the village.

They sat together on the bank. The healer motioned for silence. For a long time, they simply watched. The river danced as it moved, tumbling over stones, swirling around obstacles, sparkling wherever sunlight touched its surface.

Finally, the healer spoke softly. *"Look. The river does not resist the stones in its path. It flows around them, carrying its song forward. It does not stagnate, for it is always moving. And because it flows, it remains alive, clear, and full of light."*

The patient's eyes followed the current. Slowly, his breath deepened.

"Your blood is a river too," she continued. *"When it grows sluggish, your body forgets what the Earth has always known: to move is to live. If you would heal, remember the river. Drink fresh water, let it wash through you. Move your body as the river moves: walk, stretch, and breathe deeply. In this way, your blood will remember its rhythm, and your spirit will remember its light."*

The man wept quietly, not only because of her words, but because in that moment he felt the river speaking through her. He felt his own body mirror the flow, his heart a current, his veins small streams, his breath a wind stirring the surface.

When he rose to leave, he placed his hand on his chest and whispered, *"I will remember the river."*

In the days that followed, he often walked to the stream, drinking its calm water, breathing in its rhythm, and moving in harmony with its flow. His body grew lighter, his energy returned, and gratitude welled within him like a spring.

Years later, when others came to him weary and burdened, he shared the same wisdom he had been given:

"When your blood is sluggish, sit by a river. Watch as it flows around stones, sparkling with light. Drink water. Move your body. And let your blood remember the river."

Guided Meditation – Earth-Body Mirror

1. Lie down or sit comfortably.
2. Inhale deeply, feeling your body as a landscape.
3. Imagine:
    - **Bones** = mountains
    - **Blood** = rivers
    - **Breath** = wind

    - **Heart** = fire at the core
    - **Skin** = soil
4. Whisper: *"I am the Earth in human form."*
5. Rest in stillness, letting body and planet reflect one another.

Practices for Step 6

- **Earth-Body Scan:** As you breathe, honor each part of your body as part of Earth.
- **Chakra–Earth Alignment:** Visualize your chakras connected to Earth's sacred sites (Mount Shasta, Uluru, Glastonbury, etc.).
- **Eating as Communion:** Before meals, pause. Whisper: *"As I eat, Earth becomes me. I am Earth nourishing herself."*
- **Forest Breathing:** Sit near trees. Inhale deeply, feeling oxygen enter you. Exhale, offering carbon dioxide back. Whisper: *"We breathe as one."*

Journaling Pages

- Which part of your body feels most connected to Earth? Why?
- How might caring for your body also be caring for Earth?
- Write a love letter to your body as if to Earth herself.
- Imagine Earth speaking through your body. What would she say?

Poetic Closing

Skin of soil, bones of stone, blood of rivers, breath of sky, heart of fire.

I am the Earth. The Earth is me. The mirror is whole.

Every step I take, the ground remembers. Every breath I draw, the forests answer. Every beat of my heart echoes the molten core, steady, alive, eternal.

I am not separate. I am not small. I am woven of stars and soil, of tides and lightning, of mountain and wind.

When I bend, I am the willow. When I break, I am the stone that endures. When I flow, I am the river returning to the sea. When I shine, I am the fire at the heart of all things.

The Earth sings in my veins. The cosmos breathes in my chest. The great mirror shatters every illusion of division, and I remember that I was never apart. I was always whole.

Skin of soil, bones of stone, blood of rivers, breath of sky, heart of fire.

I am the Earth. The Earth is me. The mirror is whole. And in this wholeness, I rise, I shine, I belong.

STEP 7:

THE HEARTBEAT OF GAIA

Invocation

Pulse of the Mother, drum of creation, beat within me, beat around me, beat through me.

I walk in rhythm with your eternal song.

The Rhythm Beneath Our Feet

Every living being carries a rhythm. Your heart beats its steady drum within your chest. Your breath rises and falls like tides. Even your brain hums with waves, pulses of thought, memory, and dream.

So too does the Earth. Beneath forests and deserts, beneath seas and mountains, there is a subtle, ancient rhythm —a great heartbeat that has pulsed since the dawn of life. It is the soundless drum that steadies the world, the vibration that holds all creatures in its embrace.

To feel this rhythm is to remember: you are not separate from Earth's song. You are not a lone instrument playing in isolation. You are a note within her symphony, rising and falling in harmony with every other living being.

When you pause, when you listen, you may notice it, the thrum beneath your feet, the cadence in your chest, the way waves, winds, and seasons all move to a hidden tempo. This is the rhythm of Gaia, and it beats within you as surely as it beats within the Earth.

Myths and Sacred Traditions of the Heartbeat

Across cultures, the pulse of Earth has always been remembered through drums, chants, and stories.

- **The Drum of the Mother (Native America):** In many traditions, the drum is referred to as the heartbeat of Mother Earth. In ceremony, its rhythm aligns people with her pulse, opening the body to healing and the spirit to harmony.
- **The Cosmic Sound (Hindu Tradition):** Creation itself began with Om, the primordial vibration, the first pulse of existence. This sound is the universal heartbeat, resonating through every atom.
- **African Drumming (West Africa):** The djembe does not speak only for entertainment; it carries ancestral voices, calling communities into unity. The drumbeat is a combination of prayer, story, and heartbeat.
- **Sámi Shamans (Northern Europe):** The frame drum, steady and deep, guides shamans between worlds. Its rhythm is the thread that keeps them tethered to Earth as they journey beyond.
- **Māori Breath of Life:** For the Māori, Earth's pulse is felt in the tides, the winds, and the breath itself. Human life is but one rhythm in the greater cycle of Gaia's breathing.

Across traditions, the lesson is the same: The drumbeat is never separate from the Earth. It is her voice, her pulse, her presence calling us into rhythm with her.

Sacred-Historical Practices

Humanity has always sought to echo Gaia's pulse through ritual and practice.

- **Drumming Circles:** Across the world, people gather around fire, beating drums in unison until individual rhythms dissolve into one shared heartbeat. Healing, prayer, and unity arise through resonance.
- **Chanting and Song:** From Vedic hymns to Gregorian chants, humans have utilized sound to align themselves with the cosmic rhythm, allowing their voice to become part of the universal pulse.

- **Dancing in Rhythm:** Sufi whirling, African dances, and Native American powwows are all ways of embodying Earth's rhythm, letting the body become the drum and the heart the song.
- **Heartbeat Ceremonies:** Many traditions begin gatherings with a steady drum, reminding all present that before words, before action, there is rhythm, the pulse of life itself.

These practices were not entertainment. They were acts of remembrance, ways of coming home to the Mother's heartbeat.

Science Echoes the Heartbeat

Modern science, too, affirms what the ancients knew.

Schumann Resonance: Earth's electromagnetic field resonates at ~7.83 Hz, often called the *"heartbeat of the Earth."* Remarkably, this matches the brain's alpha-theta waves, which are associated with states of meditation, creativity, and calm.

- **Brainwave Entrainment:** Steady drumming can shift brainwaves into relaxed or trance states, synchronizing human minds with Earth's natural frequency.
- **Heart Coherence:** Research shows that when people drum, sing, or meditate together, their heartbeats synchronize. Entire communities literally *"beat as one."*
- **Geomagnetic Storms:** When solar flares disrupt Earth's electromagnetic field, humans experience it through restlessness, vivid dreams, and mood shifts. Our bodies are tuned to Gaia's pulse, whether we realize it or not.

Science confirms what the story has always told us: Earth beats, and we beat with her.

The Spiritual Meaning

To feel Gaia's heartbeat is to remember you are never alone. You are carried by her rhythm, sustained by her pulse, cradled by a love older than memory.

Her beat teaches:

- Stability, the rhythm never ceases, reminding you that life holds steady even through change.
- Unity, all hearts, all breaths, are tuned to one great pulse. You are connected to every living being.
- Guidance, when to rest, when to act, when to release, all can be felt by aligning with her rhythm.

When you ignore the pulse, life feels chaotic, frantic, disconnected. But when you return to it, through drum, breath, silence, or song, you find balance. The chaos softens, the noise fades, and life begins to flow again.

To live as an Earth Keeper is to walk not only by clocks and schedules, but by Gaia's eternal drum. Her heartbeat is your anchor, your compass, your song.

And when you lean into it, you discover the truth: You were never separate. You have constantly been beating in time.

Stories of the Pulse: The Ceremony of Unity

The people gathered in a wide clearing, where firelight flickered against the faces of elders, children, mothers, and hunters. At the center of the circle sat a great drum, its skin stretched tight across a carved wooden frame. The fire crackled, and the night air hummed with expectancy.

When the elder lifted his hand, silence fell. Then the first strike came, boom, deep and steady, like the pulse of the Earth itself. The sound rolled through the ground and into the bodies of those gathered. Each heartbeat quickened, then softened, attuning to the great rhythm.

At first, each person sang their own song. Some voices were loud and piercing, some soft as whispers. Some sang words, others only tones. For a while, the songs clashed, overlapping without order, each voice holding tightly to its own way.

But the drum continued, boom, boom, boom, unwavering, steady as the heartbeat of Mother Earth. Slowly, the people began to listen. One by one, voices bent toward the drum, finding the spaces between beats, weaving themselves into the rhythm. Discord gave way to harmony.

Soon, the circle was filled with one great sound: many voices, yet one song. Children swayed, elders tapped their feet, mothers and fathers lifted their hands to the sky. The air vibrated with something greater than music; it was belonging, communion, remembrance.

When the last note faded into the night, silence returned, thick and sweet. The elder stood, his face lit by the embers. He spoke slowly, his words carrying the weight of generations.

"This, " he said, placing his hand upon the drum, *"is how life works. We do not need to be the same. Each of you carries your own song, your own path, your own truth. But when we remember the same heartbeat, when we walk in rhythm with the Mother, our differences no longer divide us. They become harmony. "*

The people bowed their heads, tears shining in some eyes. They had not only sung together, they had remembered themselves as part of something vast, ancient, and alive.

That night, as they returned to their homes, the beat of the drum lingered in their bodies. Long after the fire had died, the memory of the rhythm guided their steps, reminding them that unity does not erase difference; it weaves difference into beauty.

And from that day on, whenever conflict or sorrow arose, someone would strike the drum, calling the people back, not to sameness, but to the heartbeat they all shared.

The Sleepless Woman

For many years, a woman carried the weight of sleepless nights. No matter how tired her body felt, her mind raced like a restless animal, chasing worries, circling through regrets, leaping toward fears of tomorrow. She tried every remedy she knew: teas, pills, meditations, and even long walks before bed. Still, when darkness fell, she lay awake, staring at the ceiling, her heart pounding louder than the night.

One day, exhausted and desperate, she moved to a small cabin at the edge of a forest, hoping that the quiet might help her find rest. But the first nights there brought no peace. Though the city's noise was gone, her anxiety followed her. The silence felt sharp, almost unbearable, and she wondered if she had only traded one kind of torment for another.

But then something began to shift.

Lying awake one night with her window open, she noticed the sounds outside were not empty. Crickets were pulsing in steady waves. There was the gentle sway of branches creaking against each other. There was the hush of wind moving like breath through the trees. Beneath it all, a low and steady rhythm, ancient and unbroken, seemed to rise from the earth itself.

She closed her eyes. For the first time in many years, she let herself listen, really listen. Her own breath was jagged, out of step. Slowly, she tried to match the rhythm of the crickets. Inhale, exhale. Then she felt her chest rise and fall like the trees swaying in the wind. She imagined her heartbeat syncing with the deep thrum of the earth beneath her cabin floor.

Something softened. Her racing thoughts, once like storms, began to dissolve into the rhythm all around her. Her body, long trapped in tension, loosened into the flow. For the first time in years, she drifted into a peaceful, deep, and whole sleep.

In the mornings that followed, she woke renewed, the dark circles under her eyes fading, her spirit lighter. Night after night, she returned to the forest's rhythms, not resisting her wakefulness but listening until her body remembered its belonging to the great pulse of life.

Later, when she spoke of her healing, she said, *"It wasn't silence that healed me, it was rhythm. The rhythm of the world reminded my body of what it had forgotten: that I am part of the great song. And in that song, I could finally rest. "*

From then on, she no longer feared the night. She welcomed it as a teacher, a place where rhythm whispered her back into harmony. And whenever she lay down, she placed her hand on her chest and listened for the truth she had learned: that every heart, when it remembers the Earth's pulse, can find its way back to peace.

Guided Meditation – Attuning to Gaia's Beat

1. Sit or lie on the Earth. Place one hand on your heart, one on the soil.
2. Breathe slowly. Imagine your heartbeat syncing with Earth beneath you.
3. Whisper: *"Mother, align me with your pulse. "*
4. Stay in silence. Feel your rhythm merge with hers.
5. When ready, thank her: *"Your song is my song. I walk in your rhythm. "*

Practices for Step 7

- **Drum Journey:** Strike a drum or clap steadily for 15 minutes. Let the rhythm carry you into stillness.

- **Breath of Resonance:** Inhale for 6 counts, exhale for 6. Let your heart settle into coherence.
- **Walking the Beat:** Walk outdoors, letting your steps match your heartbeat.
- **Heartbeat Circle:** Sit with others, place hands on your hearts, and breathe together until rhythms synchronize.

Journaling Pages

- When have you felt *"in sync"* with life? Describe the moment.
- Which rhythms, sunrise, tides, seasons, song, guide you most?
- How might you live more by Gaia's rhythm than by artificial time?
- If Earth drummed through you, what song would she play?

STEP 8:

HEALING WITH THE EARTH

Invocation

Mother of waters, Father of stones, Spirit of air, Fire of renewal,

I open myself to your medicine. Heal me as I heal you. Together we rise whole.

The Circle of Healing

The Earth is not only our home, she is our healer. She offers her medicine constantly, whether we notice it or not.

Every breath of fresh air that clears your thoughts, every sip of cool water that soothes your thirst, every walk beneath trees that steadies your heart, these are not accidents of biology. They are Gaia's medicine, freely offered, an ancient and ongoing conversation between body and Earth.

But healing is not one-way. For too long, humanity has taken from the Earth without giving back. We have received her rivers, her forests, her minerals, her air, and often forgotten to return gratitude, care, or balance. The wisdom of the Earth Keeper reminds us: healing flows in both directions.

When we breathe clean air, we heal. When we plant trees, the Earth heals. When we drink fresh water, we are restored. When we protect rivers, they flow clear again. This is the sacred reciprocity at the heart of the Earth Keeper's path: to receive and to give, to be healed and to heal, to live in the circle of exchange that sustains all life.

Healing is never separate; it is a circle. When you heal, the Earth heals. When the Earth heals, you heal.

Myths and Sacred Traditions of Healing

Across cultures, Earth has always been known as the great physician:

- **The Ganges (Hindu):** The sacred river Ganga is said to descend from heaven to cleanse karma and heal the soul. Bathing in her waters is believed to rejuvenate both the spirit and the body.
- **Lourdes (Christian, France):** Millions of pilgrims visit the springs of Lourdes, where countless healings have been reported, and faith itself becomes part of the cure.
- **Celtic Holy Wells:** Springs dedicated to Brigid were visited for the purposes of improving eyesight, enhancing fertility, and promoting recovery from wounds. Pilgrims tied ribbons to nearby trees, leaving prayers for renewal.
- **Incan Healing Ceremonies:** Shamans offered coca leaves, songs, and breath to Pachamama, asking for health in exchange for gratitude. Healing was never *"taken"* but shared.
- **Aboriginal Healing Songs (Australia):** Songs of the Dreamtime were sung over the sick, reconnecting the person to land, ancestors, and spirit. Healing flowed through the relationship.
- **Navajo Blessingway:** These ceremonies restored hózhó, harmony and beauty, realigning the person with Earth's order, which is the root of health.

From wells to rivers, from chants to ceremonies, the pattern is clear: humans have always turned to Earth for healing, and Earth has always responded when approached with reverence.

Sacred-Historical Practices

Healing with the Earth was not a metaphor; it was a lived experience.

- **Sweat Lodges (Indigenous Americas):** Stones, fire, steam, and prayer brought people into the womb of Earth, cleansing body, mind, and soul.
- **Fire Ceremonies (Andes, Vedic India):** Flames symbolized transformation, burning away heaviness, and renewing the life force.
- **Herbal Medicine (Worldwide):** Plants have long been revered as the children of the Earth, each carrying a unique spirit and a healing gift.
- **Pilgrimages:** People walked to shrines, wells, and mountains not only for worship, but also for the recovery of health, their bodies healed by the journey, and their spirits healed by devotion.

Healing was never seen as something separate from place. To heal was to reconnect with the land.

Science Echoes the Medicine

Modern research now confirms what ancient wisdom always held:

- **Forest Bathing (Japan):** Time among trees lowers stress hormones, steadies the heart, and boosts immunity. Trees release phytoncides, compounds that have a strengthening effect on the body.
- **Earthing:** Walking barefoot on soil balances the body's electrical charge, reducing inflammation, calming the nervous system, and improving sleep.
- **Ocean and Waterfalls:** The negative ions released by waves and falling water increase serotonin, thereby lifting mood and energy.
- **Soil and the Mind:** A bacterium in healthy soil, Mycobacterium vaccae, activates serotonin pathways, helping ease depression.

Science rediscovers what indigenous people never forgot: Gaia is medicine, and we are designed to be in relationship with her.

The Spiritual Meaning

To allow the Earth to heal you is to remember that you are not separate, not alone, not cut off from the greater body of life. You are a child returning to the embrace of your Mother.

Yet healing is not meant to be taken like a possession. It is not a commodity. Healing is meant to be received in reverence and given back in love. When you restore balance within yourself, you become a healing presence for Earth. When you protect and nurture Earth, you restore balance within yourself.

This is the teaching of reciprocity: to heal with the Earth, not just from her.

The invitation is simple yet profound:

- Walk with gratitude.
- Drink with reverence.
- Rest in forests as though they were temples.
- Offer back care, prayer, and protection in return for all you receive.

Healing is not passive. It is active, relational, and alive. The Earth offers you her medicine, and your task is to live in such a way that she, too, is restored.

Stories of Healing: The Clay of Renewal

An elder once gathered his people by the fire and spoke of a time of great trial. A strange illness had spread through the village, leaving many weak, feverish, and unable to rise from their beds. The healers tried all they knew, herbs, prayers, chants, and smoke, but still the sickness lingered.

At last, when remedies seemed exhausted, they turned to the river, whose waters had always nourished them, and to the clay that lined its banks. The people remembered that Earth herself is the first medicine, and so they humbled themselves before her.

They dug their hands into the cool, damp clay, lifting it with reverence as if lifting the flesh of the Mother herself. They covered their bodies in it, faces, arms, chests, and legs, until each one was coated in the Earth's skin. Together they sat in silence, waiting.

As the clay began to dry, the elder said, they felt something extraordinary. It was as though the heaviness of their sickness, the fever in their blood, and the ache in their bones were being drawn outward, absorbed by the cool, embracing Earth. Their skin tingled. Their breath slowed. The weight that pressed upon their spirits seemed to loosen.

When at last they entered the river and let the waters wash them clean, they watched the clay dissolve and swirl away. With it, they felt their sickness lessen, their bodies lighter, their hearts steadier.

The elder looked around the circle of listeners, his eyes bright with memory. *"The Earth absorbed our sickness,"* he said softly. *"She did not turn us away. She took what we could not carry on our own. But because we loved her, we knew not to abandon her with our burdens. We sang to her, songs of gratitude and blessing, so that she would not carry our pain in silence. Our voices became medicine for her, as she had been medicine for us."*

He paused, then added, *"This is the great exchange: to take, and also to give. To be healed, and to heal. The Earth does not belong to us, nor do we belong apart from her. We are woven together. She takes our sickness into her body, and we give her our songs, our care, our devotion. In this way, both are renewed."*

The people listening that night felt the truth of his words ripple through them like the river's current. Some had never considered healing as a mutual process. They had only thought of the Earth as a giver, and themselves as receivers. But now they saw a greater truth: healing was a circle.

And so the story was passed on: that the clay of the Earth is not only soil, not only matter, it is compassion made visible. It is her willingness to take what burdens us, so long as we return to her not with indifference, but with love.

From then on, whenever sickness or sorrow weighed upon the people, they remembered the elder's teaching. They turned to the Earth, not only for healing, but also for relationships. They prayed as they gathered clay. They sang as they washed it away. And in the rhythm of giving and receiving, they remembered what it meant to live in balance.

The Tree as Therapist

There was once a woman living in a world that never seemed to stop moving. She worked long hours, her phone buzzing constantly, her nights restless with worry. Anxiety had become her constant companion, tightening her chest, stealing her breath, clouding her thoughts. She tried therapy, medication, meditation apps, but nothing seemed to reach the place inside her that ached for peace.

One afternoon, feeling overwhelmed, she wandered into a nearby park. Without planning it, she sat down beneath a great oak tree whose wide branches stretched like welcoming arms. She leaned her back against its trunk, feeling the rough bark through her clothes. It was not a conscious choice, just a place to catch her breath.

At first, she thought it silly. *"What am I doing? Sitting under a tree as if it can help me?"* she muttered. But the oak did not answer. It simply stood, rooted and patient, as it had for centuries. It did not judge. It did not hurry her. It did not ask her to be different from what she was.

So she kept returning. Day after day, she came to the oak. Sometimes she sat in silence. Sometimes she scrolled her phone, pretending not to notice, and she felt calmer there. Sometimes she leaned against its trunk and closed her eyes, listening to the wind whispering through its leaves.

Over time, something subtle began to shift. The tree became a steady presence in her chaotic life. Unlike people, it never interrupted her or offered advice she could not follow. Unlike her racing mind, it did not pressure her to perform, fix, or prove. It simply was. Strong. Silent. Present.

One afternoon, as she sat in the shade, all the weight she had been carrying seemed to press down at once. Tears welled up, and before she could stop herself, she burst into sobs, loud, unrestrained, unguarded. She pressed her forehead against the bark and let it all pour out: the fear, the exhaustion, the loneliness she had hidden even from herself.

The tree did not move. It did not recoil. It held her the only way a tree can, by being steady, rooted, unwavering. And in that stillness, she felt something she hadn't felt in years: relief.

Later, she would tell a friend, *"The tree was my counselor. It listened without words, it held me without arms. It stayed until I could hold myself again."*

From then on, she no longer saw her visits as silly. They became sacred. The oak was her therapist, her anchor, her witness. And though it never spoke, she came to understand its teaching: that healing often comes not from solving, but from being held, by silence, by presence, by something larger than yourself.

And in time, she realized something even more profound: the oak had not only healed her. By giving it her tears, her trust, her presence, she too had honored the tree. She watered its roots with her grief, and in exchange, it had given her the medicine of stillness. It was a relationship of reciprocity, as all true healing is.

The woman still carries her anxiety from time to time, but she no longer feels alone with it. She holds the oak within her, a reminder that strength does not mean speed, and healing does not mean perfection. Sometimes, it means finding something that can hold you until you remember how to hold yourself.

Guided Meditation – Receiving and Returning

1. Sit outdoors or imagine a natural place.
2. Place your hands on the Earth. Whisper: *"Mother, I receive your healing."*
3. Inhale deeply, imagining light rising from soil, water, or air into your body.
4. Let the light fill every cell, washing away heaviness.
5. When you feel complete, place your hands again on the ground. Whisper: *"Mother, I return healing to you."*
6. Imagine love and gratitude flowing from your heart into the Earth.

Practices for Step 8

- **Elemental Healing:** Each day, spend time with one element, Earth (barefoot walking), Water (mindful drinking), Fire (candle gazing), Air (breath meditation). Notice its medicine.
- **Song of Healing:** Sing softly to the land, offering your voice as medicine in return.
- **Healing Exchange:** After receiving comfort from a place (a river, a forest, a stone), leave an offering, a prayer, a flower, or an act of care.
- **Body as Offering:** Care for your own health (sleep, food, rest) as a way of offering vitality back to Earth.

Journaling Pages

- When has nature healed you most deeply? Describe the experience.
- Which element feels most healing to you right now? Why?

- How can you give healing back to the Earth each day?
- If you were a medicine for the Earth, what healing would you offer?

Poetic Closing

Waters that cleanse, stones that ground, air that revives, fire that renews. You heal me, Mother.

With every sip of spring water, you wash away my heaviness. With every river's song, you remind me to flow, to move, to release. With every drop of rain upon my skin, I feel the world's tears and know I am not alone.

With every stone beneath my feet, you steady me. You whisper of patience, of ages older than memory. Your mountains rise in my spine, your cliffs give me courage, and in your quiet strength I find my own.

With every breath of air, you awaken me. You rush through me as wind through branches, filling my lungs with clarity, sweeping away the shadows of doubt. Invisible, yet undeniable, you teach me the gift of what cannot be seen but must be trusted.

With every flame that dances, you ignite me anew. You burn away the husks of what no longer serves, you warm my coldest nights, you shine light into my darkness until I remember I, too, am fire.

You heal me, Mother, in ways both vast and tender, in the silence of stones, in the laughter of streams, in the wild breath of wind, in the fierce embrace of flame.

And I, your child, vow not only to receive but to return. I offer you my gratitude, my song, my footsteps in reverence. I offer you my care, my choices, my love alive in action. I vow to be part of your healing as you are part of mine.

For we are not two, we are one. When I drink, you drink. When I breathe, you breathe. When I burn with love, your light spreads further into the world.

Waters that cleanse, stones that ground, air that revives, fire that renews.

I walk in your circle. I live in your rhythm. I rise in your wholeness. You heal me, Mother, and through me, may you be healed too.

STEP 9:

THE SHIFTING FREQUENCIES OF NOW

Invocation

Waves of light, currents of sound, heartbeat quickening, time unfolding.

Mother, I rise with you. I attune to your song. I walk in your frequency.

The Great Shift

The Earth is changing. She is no longer the same as she was even a generation ago. Her rhythms are quickening, her vibrations rising, her pulse growing stronger with every passing season.

For some, this change feels unsettling. Time seems to slip faster through the fingers. Old ways no longer fit. Bodies feel fatigued, emotions heightened, and dreams strange and vivid. For others, the shift feels like clarity, awakening, and expansion. Doors of perception open, synchronicities multiply, intuition sharpens.

Both experiences are authentic, for we are living at a threshold, the Shifting Frequencies of Now.

The ancients foresaw this moment in prophecy. Modern science measures it in data. The soul feels it in restlessness, in longing, in the deep sense that something vast is unfolding.

To live in this time is to live in a state of transformation. It is to walk through fire, but also to walk into light.

Prophecies of Transformation

Throughout time, cultures across the world spoke of a moment when the Earth and her people would change together:

- **Mayan Calendar:** The end of the 13th baktun in 2012 was never meant to signal destruction, but rather renewal, the turning of the ages, and the rebirth of human consciousness into a higher octave.
- **Hopi Prophecy:** The elders spoke of a Great Purification, a pivotal moment where humanity must choose between harmony and destruction. Those who walk in balance, they said, will seed the new world.
- **Andean Q'ero (Peru):** The prophecy of Pachakuti foretells a great turning, when the world is set upright again, and humans remember their sacred role as guardians and keepers of balance.
- **Christian Revelation:** *"A new heaven and a new Earth"* is promised, not annihilation, but divine transformation, where love restores creation.
- **Hindu Yugas:** The Kali Yuga, the age of shadow, is destined to give way to Satya Yuga, the age of truth, when humanity returns to dharma, light, and balance.

Though their languages differ, the message is the same: we are in a time of rising frequency, and the Earth is calling her children to awaken.

Sacred-Historical Practices of Alignment

When the ground of reality trembled beneath them, humans have always turned to ritual to find their center.

- **Fasts and Vision Quests:** To clear the old, to empty oneself so new energies may enter.
- **Sun Dances and Fire Ceremonies:** To align body and spirit with the cycles of cosmic renewal.

- **Mantras and Chants:** Repetition of sound frequencies to bring the soul into harmony with the universal pulse.
- **Seasonal Festivals:** Solstices, equinoxes, and harvest rites kept entire communities in rhythm with Earth's shifting tides.

The ancients knew that when Earth shifts, humanity must move with her, not through resistance, but through reverence.

Science Echoes the Shift

Even modern science has begun to trace the outlines of this significant change:

- **Schumann Resonance:** Once stable at ~7.83 Hz, Earth's electromagnetic *"heartbeat"* now shows spikes and fluctuations. Mystics call this her quickening.
- **Solar Activity:** Solar flares and geomagnetic storms alter the Earth's magnetosphere, and humans experience it through mood swings, sleep disturbances, bursts of energy, or heightened dreams.
- **Heart–Earth Synchrony:** Studies show human heart rhythms align with Earth's electromagnetic field. As Gaia shifts, so do our own pulses.
- **Time Perception:** Increasingly, people report that time feels accelerated. Neuroscience speaks of attention shifts, but mystics whisper of frequency rising.

Science and spirit converge on the same truth: Gaia is ascending, and we are rising with her.

The Spiritual Meaning

The Shifting Frequencies of Now are not punishment. They are invited.

- Old systems crumble because they are built on fear, and fear cannot hold in higher frequencies of love.
- Old patterns dissolve because they no longer resonate with who we are becoming.
- Souls awaken because Gaia herself is calling them back to remembrance, tuning them to her rising song.

To resist this change is to suffer, clinging to structures already fading. To surrender is to rise, to allow yourself to be carried by the wave into a greater becoming.

This shift calls for trust: trust in the body, trust in the Earth, trust in the process of renewal. Just as the caterpillar cannot remain when the butterfly is ready, humanity cannot remain what it was when Gaia herself is ascending.

The invitation is to align, attune, awaken, to live not by the clock of fear, but by the frequency of love.

Stories of the Shift: The Elder's Teaching

The people had gathered in the village square, troubled by the changes that were unfolding around them. The seasons no longer felt the same, the air carried strange tensions, and life itself seemed to be moving faster than their hearts could follow. Some whispered of fear, others of endings, and many felt lost.

An elder, his hair white as winter snow, stood before them. His eyes, however, were bright with the fire of knowing. He raised his hand for silence, and when the people grew still, he began to speak.

"The river is flowing fast," he said. *"Faster than many of you have ever known. Its waters are swollen with change, with the breaking of old ways and the birth of new. Some of you will be afraid. You will cling to the banks, holding tight to what you know, though the earth crumbles beneath your grip. You will exhaust yourselves in*

resistance, shouting at the current as though you could command it to stop. "

He paused and let the weight of his words sink in. Around him, people exchanged anxious glances, for each one had felt the pull of this river of change in their own lives.

"But the wise, " the elder continued, *"the wise will not cling. They will let go. They will step into the rushing water and move into the center of the stream, where the current is strongest. At first, it may seem frightening, for the river will carry you swiftly, and you will not know every bend ahead. Yet in the center, you will find your freedom. You will be carried not by your fear, but by the river's own knowing. "*

A child raised her hand timidly. *"Grandfather, "* she asked, *"what if the river carries us where we do not want to go? "*

The elder smiled gently. *"Little one, the river has always known the way. It flows to the great ocean, where all rivers return. You may not see the path from where you stand, but the river remembers. It was carved by time itself, shaped by mountains, guided by valleys. Its course is wiser than our fear. To trust the river is to trust life itself. "*

The people listened in silence. Some felt their fear ease, others felt tears rise, and many felt a stirring of courage within their hearts.

"And so I tell you this, " the elder said. *"Do not waste your strength clinging to the banks. Do not fight the current with anger or despair. Step into the flow. Sing as you are carried. Help one another when the waters feel strong. For this is not a river of destruction, it is a river of renewal. It is carrying us into a world yet to be born. "*

Then he lifted his head and spoke one final truth:

"The time of standing still has ended. The time of remembering has begun. The river is moving, and so must we. Let go, beloved ones. Trust the current. The river knows the way. "

A Modern Awakening

There was once a man who carried the constant weight of anxiety. His chest felt tight, his sleep restless, his thoughts scattered. Some days, he wondered if something was wrong with him, for even when life was calm around him, storms raged within.

One evening, curious and desperate for answers, he began reading about the Earth's changes. He learned that when the Sun releases flares, Earth's magnetic field trembles. Some call these geomagnetic storms. Most people pay little attention, but the man noticed something strange: on those very days, his body felt different. His heart raced, his skin tingled, his dreams grew vivid.

At first, he feared the worst. *"Something must be wrong with me,"* he thought. But instead of running from it, he decided to sit with it. Each time the storms came, he set aside moments of quiet, closing his eyes, breathing slowly, and listening.

To his surprise, instead of collapsing into panic, he began to feel something else. A spaciousness. A clarity. A presence that felt larger than himself. At times, images flashed before him like visions, symbols, and colors, offering insights into his life. At other times, there was only calm, as though the storm outside had tuned the storm inside.

He began to keep a journal. The more he practiced, the more he noticed a pattern: when Earth's fields shifted, his own body shifted too. What once felt like sickness now felt like resonance. What once seemed like weakness became an awakening.

He wrote: *"At first I thought I was sick. Then I realized I was tuning. My body was adjusting to Gaia's new song."*

From that moment on, he no longer feared the storms. Instead, he welcomed them as teachers. He realized that his sensitivity, once his greatest burden, was also his greatest gift. While others rushed through life unaware, he was learning to feel the heartbeat of the Earth herself.

And his lesson was simple, yet profound: we are not separate from the Earth. When she shifts, we shift. When her song rises, our bodies must learn new harmonies. The storms were not punishments. They were invitations to awaken, to align, to remember that humanity's story is woven into the song of Gaia.

Guided Meditation – Attuning to Now

1. Sit quietly, feet on the ground, hands on your heart.
2. Breathe slowly, imagining Earth's heartbeat beneath you.
3. Visualize waves of light rising from the Earth, entering your body.
4. Whisper: *"I rise with you, Gaia. I attune to your frequency."*
5. Rest, allowing sensations, visions, or calm to flow.

Practices for Step 9

- **Release Ritual:** Write what no longer serves. Burn or bury it, releasing it into Earth's transformation.
- **Frequency Breath:** Inhale for 8 counts, exhale for 8, aligning with Gaia's rhythm.
- **Light Ripple:** Visualize your body glowing, sending ripples of light outward to all beings.
- **Daily Alignment:** Each morning, whisper: *"Mother, I align with your song today."*

Journaling Pages

- What changes in your body, emotions, or dreams signal Earth's shifting frequency?
- What old patterns are you being called to release?
- What does *"rising frequency"* mean to you personally?
- How can you align your daily rhythm with Gaia's pulse?

Poetic Closing

The river flows faster, the drum beats louder, the light grows brighter.

Do not cling. The banks will crumble. The old ways cannot hold.

Do not fear. The current is not your enemy. It is your passage, your teacher, your guide.

Let go. Step into the center of the stream. Feel the water carry you, feel the rhythm steady you, feel the song awaken you.

Rise. Rise with the river that remembers the ocean. Rise with the drum that remembers the heartbeat of the Mother. Rise with the light that remembers the stars from which you came.

The world is not ending. It is becoming. You are not drowning. You are being reborn.

So lift your voice, beloved one. Sing as you are carried. Dance as you are transformed. Trust the flow, trust the rhythm, trust the fire.

For the river flows faster, the drum beats louder, the light grows brighter, and you, child of Earth, are rising with them, sing.

The Earth is shifting, and she carries you with her.

STEP 10:

THE CIRCLE OF KEEPERS

Invocation

Ancestors and descendants, elders and children, shamans and saints, healers and dreamers.

I take my place in the circle. I stand among you. The fire is unbroken.

The Lineage of Light

No one walks the path of the Earth Keeper alone. From the beginning of time, there have always been those who remembered.

The dreamers who looked at the stars and listened for meaning. The shamans who spoke with rivers and mountains. The priestesses who guarded temples of fire and moonlight. The farmers who planted with reverence for the soil. The storytellers who carried memory across generations. The healers who mended not only bodies but spirits. The visionaries who saw beyond the present moment into a future of possibility.

They are the Circle of Keepers, the eternal family who carry Earth's wisdom from age to age.

When you step onto this path, you are not entering emptiness. You are joining a circle that has always been waiting for you. You do not stand alone. You stand hand in hand with ancestors who walked before you and with descendants who will follow after you. You are flame in a fire that has never gone out.

Myths and Sacred Traditions of the Circle

Across cultures and centuries, the circle has always been a symbol of belonging, equality, and wholeness.

- **Council Fires (Indigenous North America):** Tribes gathered in circles around the fire where every voice was heard, and no one sat above another. The circle itself was the teacher, reminding the people that all are vital to the whole.
- **Druidic Groves (Celtic Europe):** In sacred groves, Druids formed circles to align with the sun, moon, and seasons. The circle reflected the cosmos, no beginning, no end.
- **Andean Elders (Peru):** Altomisayoq shamans hold ceremonies in circles, with each participant serving as a bridge between worlds, each holding responsibility for maintaining balance.
- **Buddhist Sangha (Asia):** The community is itself a sacred refuge. No awakening is possible alone; enlightenment blossoms through the circle of practice.
- **Christian Mystics:** Early monks spoke of the *"great cloud of witnesses"*, a living circle of saints and souls surrounding and sustaining the faithful.

Across traditions, the lesson is the same: the circle means unity. In the circle, no one is higher, no one is lower. All belong.

Sacred-Historical Practices of Community

Throughout history, people lived and thrived in circles.

- **Ritual Circles:** From stone monuments to fire gatherings, communities formed rings to reflect the cosmic order above.
- **Shared Meals:** Feasts were more than food; they were ceremonies of gratitude and belonging, where every person shared equally.
- **Elders' Councils:** Wisdom was passed in circles, story to story, so that memory and guidance flowed without interruption.

- **Initiation Circles:** To be welcomed into adulthood or healing was to be placed in the circle of responsibility, no longer separate but woven into the whole.

Community was never optional. It was the ground of survival, the heartbeat of culture, and the very fabric of the sacred.

Science Echoes the Circle

Modern research affirms what the ancients lived.

- **Resonance in Groups:** Studies show that during rituals, drumming, or meditation, heartbeats and brainwaves synchronize. The circle literally brings bodies into harmony.
- **Social Neuroscience:** Humans are wired for connection. Isolation weakens health, while a strong community boosts immunity, resilience, and longevity.
- **Ancestral Memory (Epigenetics):** Science reveals that trauma and healing are passed through DNA. The circle of ancestors lives within your very body, shaping your destiny.
- **Collective Consciousness:** Group meditations have been shown to reduce conflict and crime. When people gather with shared intention, the world itself responds.

Science whispers what spirit has always shouted: the circle heals. When we join it, we align with life's deepest patterns.

The Spiritual Meaning

The Circle of Keepers is not about perfection or hierarchy. It is about presence, equality, and responsibility.

To join the circle is to honor the ancestors who walked before you. To join the circle is to stand with those walking beside you. To join the circle is to prepare the way for those who will follow one day.

When you live as a Keeper, your life becomes a thread in a tapestry far larger than yourself. Your words become songs in a choir of guardians. Your choices become sparks in an eternal fire.

The circle does not ask you to be flawless. It asks you to show up. To add your voice, your light, your presence, so that together we may remember what it means to belong, not only to humanity, but to Earth herself.

Stories of the Circle: The Hidden Fire

There was a time, the elder said, when ceremony was forbidden. Drums were silenced, sacred songs were outlawed, and gathering in circles was punished. The people were told to forget their old ways, to let their prayers fade into dust.

But not all forgot.

At night, when the world slept and watchful eyes grew weary, women slipped quietly into the darkness. They carried with them not great torches or blazing hearths, but tiny sparks, a coal smuggled from a kitchen fire, a candle shielded in cupped hands, a twig of resinous pine. In hidden groves, behind barns, or in the shadow of hills, they lit their small flames.

Around these fragile lights, they whispered the old prayers, not in loud chants that might draw punishment, but in hushed voices, softer than wind in the grass. They prayed for their children, for the soil, for the waters, for the memory of what was once whole. Their songs were nearly inaudible, yet they rose like smoke, unseen but not unheard.

"Even if no one else remembered," the elder said, *"the fire remembered."*

The flames were not only of wood and ember. They were flames of memory, passed hand to hand, heart to heart. They burned in silence, but they did not die.

Through those hidden nights, the circle endured. Children sleeping in nearby homes dreamed of warmth, though they knew not why. Seeds planted in spring seemed to lean toward the prayers sung in secret. The Earth herself felt the heat of devotion, faint but unbroken.

Generations later, when it was safe again to gather openly, the people returned to the great circles of fire. They beat the drums, lifted their songs, and told the stories once more. But they all knew: it was the small fires, the hidden, trembling, defiant flames, that had kept the memory alive.

The elder smiled with eyes both fierce and tender. *"Never underestimate a small fire,"* she said. *"For one flame can carry a thousand years of prayer. One whispered word can keep a people alive. The fire remembers, even when we forget. And because the fire remembers, the circle will always endure."*

The Dream Gathering

One night, a weary seeker, burdened by doubt and loneliness, drifted into sleep. In her dream, she found herself walking across an endless plain, under a sky alive with stars. The air shimmered with a quiet expectancy, as if the whole universe was holding its breath.

At the edge of the plain, she saw firelight. Drawn toward it, she came upon a vast circle. It stretched farther than her eyes could follow, unbroken, glowing like a living ring of light. Around the circle stood countless beings, elders in flowing robes whose faces carried the lines of centuries, children with eyes bright as dawn, shamans drumming rhythms that echoed like the heartbeat of the Earth, saints cloaked in silence whose stillness spoke more than words, and ordinary people, farmers, healers, mothers, teachers, wanderers, each radiating a quiet, unmistakable glow.

The seeker hesitated at the edge, unsure if she belonged. She felt her smallness, her mistakes, the weight of her forgotten prayers. But then, as if sensing her fear, the circle shifted. A woman with hair as silver as moonlight turned and looked at her. The woman's eyes carried both fierce knowing and tender compassion. She reached out a hand, her palm warm and steady.

"You were always with us," she said, her voice like both a whisper and a bell. *"Even when you forgot, we remembered you. Even when you wandered, the circle held your place. Now you remember."*

At those words, the seeker felt her heart crack open. A flood of recognition surged through her, memories she had never lived yet somehow always carried: the smell of sacred smoke, the drumbeat of ancestors, the laughter of children not yet born. She saw her own life as a thread woven into a grand tapestry, one strand among countless others, each necessary, each luminous.

Tears streamed down her face, not of sorrow but of relief. She stepped into the circle, and as her foot touched the ground, the drums shifted, the chant deepened, and the fire blazed brighter. The circle welcomed her not as a guest, but as kin.

Then she understood: the circle was not only in her dream. It had always been here, across generations, across worlds, seen and unseen. It was the eternal gathering of all who remember the Earth, the light, the sacred. And she, like everyone, had never been outside it. She had only forgotten.

When she woke, the seeker's pillow was wet with tears, but her heart was steady and strong. She carried with her the elder's words like a living flame: *"You were always with us. Now you remember."*

And from that day forward, whenever loneliness returned, she closed her eyes, placed her hand upon her heart, and felt the circle, vast, unbroken, waiting, and alive, beating within her.

Guided Meditation – Entering the Circle

1. Sit quietly. Close your eyes.

2. Imagine a fire glowing before you.
3. See figures gathering, ancestors, elders, future generations, teachers, and unknown faces radiant with light.
4. Step into the circle. Whisper: *"I take my place among you."*
5. Feel the fire's warmth. Hear the voices rise in blessing.
6. Rest, belonging.

Practices for Step 10

- **Circle of Prayer:** Gather friends or family. Sit in a circle. Each person speaks a prayer for Earth. Hold hands, letting the energy flow.
- **Ancestral Candle:** Light a candle for your ancestors, known or unknown, who lived in reverence with Earth. Whisper thanks.
- **Future Letter:** Write to descendants or future humanity, sharing how you walk as Keeper. Bury or place it under a tree.
- **Everyday Circle:** When eating with others, form a small ritual by holding hands, sharing gratitude, and remembering the circle.

Journaling Pages

- Who in your family or ancestry embodied Earth wisdom?
- When have you felt most supported by the community?
- What gifts do you bring to the Circle of Keepers?
- How do you want to be remembered by those who come after?

Poetic Closing

The fire burns, steady, ancient, alive. It has never gone out, not through night nor storm, for it is the fire of the First Dawn, carried in hearts, carried in hands, passed from elder to child, from dreamer to seeker.

The circle holds, vast as the horizon, wider than oceans, older than time. It holds the laughter of children not yet born, the prayers of ancestors whispered into stone, the breath of every being who has ever remembered.

The ancestors sing, their voices woven in wind, their footsteps still echoing through mountains and plains. They sing of endurance, of courage, of belonging. They sing us awake, again and again.

The children listen, their eyes bright with dawn, their spirits hungry for stories that remind them who they are and why they came. They listen for our truth, and they will carry forward our songs.

The Keepers remember, remembering not only for themselves, but for the world, for the forgotten, the weary, the lost. Their remembering is a flame, a map, a promise.

The circle is unbroken. It cannot be broken. Even when scattered, we are one. Even when silenced, we endure. Even when forgotten, the circle remembers itself.

And now, I step across the threshold. I stand within the fire. I join the voices of the ancestors. I take the hands of the children. I vow to remember, to guard, to keep. For I, too, am part of the circle. And the circle is part of me.

STEP 11:

BECOMING A KEEPER

Invocation

Keeper of fire, Keeper of stone, Keeper of water, Keeper of breath, Keeper of the ancient song of Earth, I rise to the vow. I step across the threshold. I live as the guardian of Gaia, and I remember who I am.

The Threshold of Vocation

Every journey of awakening carries a moment when listening is no longer enough. You have heard the whisper in the wind, the heartbeat of the Earth beneath your feet, the stories carved in stone and sung by waters. You have seen the web of life shimmering all around you. But there comes a time when you must move beyond listening and seeing. You must become.

To become a Keeper is to stand at that threshold, the crossing point between being a witness and becoming a participant. It is the moment when you stop waiting for someone else to heal, to lead, to care, and you realize: it is my turn.

A Keeper is not crowned by kings, nor certified by institutions. There is no diploma, no outer sign. The vow is inward. It is whispered to Gaia in the silence of your heart. It is sealed not by signatures but by the way you choose to live.

The vow of a Keeper is not a vow of perfection. You will falter, forget, stumble, and rise again. The vow is not about superiority. It is about service, a life lived in reverence, with love as the compass and Earth as the teacher. To become a Keeper is to remember, and in remembering, to embody.

Myths and Sacred Traditions of Initiation

Every culture has known this truth: to walk as healer, shaman, priestess, monk, or guardian requires initiation, a passage through fire, shadow, or silence into a greater life.

- **Eleusinian Mysteries (Greece):** In ancient Greece, initiates descended into darkness, faced the silence of death, and then emerged into light. They vowed to live in harmony with the eternal cycles of death and rebirth.
- **Vision Quests (Indigenous North America):** Youth left the village to fast and pray in solitude. Alone in the wilderness, they faced fear and vision. When they returned, they were no longer the same; they came back as adults, committed to serving the people and the land.
- **Shamanic Deaths (Siberia, Amazon, Andes):** Many shamans were called not by choice but by crisis, illness, lightning, or madness. Surviving became initiation. From their wound, they emerged transformed, carrying medicine for others.
- **Mystery Schools (Egypt):** Students studied stars, geometry, sound, and silence. Their actual graduation was not knowledge but transformation; they themselves became living temples.
- **Christian Monastic Vows:** Monks and nuns stepped across thresholds into cloisters, vowing to dedicate themselves to prayer, service, and simplicity. Their lives themselves became liturgies.

Across continents and centuries, the story is the same: initiation is not given lightly. It asks you to step through death, of ego, of certainty, of old life, into new birth as a bearer of light.

Sacred-Historical Practices

The outer forms of initiation varied, but all carried the same essence: surrender, transformation, rebirth.

- Fasting and Pilgrimage, Emptying the self so the spirit could fill the body.
- Vows of Silence or Poverty, Stripping away distractions to reveal the soul's core.
- Anointing with Water or Oil, Consecrating the body as a vessel of divine purpose.
- Ceremonial Naming, Receiving a new name to mark the new life.

These acts were not symbols. They were thresholds, signaling that one life had ended and another had begun.

Science Echoes Initiation

Even modern science affirms the transformative power of vows and thresholds.

- **Neuroplasticity:** The brain rewires when we commit deeply. A vow reshapes pathways, carving new rivers of thought and action.
- **Rites of Passage Psychology:** Ritual crossings foster resilience and maturity, thereby strengthening a person's identity.
- **Sound and Intention:** Studies show that speaking vows aloud increases follow-through, words shape reality, and reality echoes words.
- **Trauma and Growth:** Many who endure crisis discover meaning and transformation. Like shamans of old, wounds become gateways to wisdom.

Science quietly affirms what spirit always knew: vows do not only change the mind, they remake the whole being.

The Spiritual Meaning

To become a Keeper is to rise into responsibility. It is to recognize that your life is no longer only your own. You belong to the Earth, and she belongs to you.

To be a Keeper means:

- To tend, to care for land, water, body, and community with reverence.
- To remember, to keep alive the truth that Earth is sacred, alive, and worthy of devotion.
- To serve, to offer your gifts without demand for recognition, only love.
- To embody, to live each day as prayer, each breath as communion, each choice as offering.

You are not asked never to falter. You are asked to keep walking. You are not asked to be perfect. You are asked to be faithful. You are not asked to save the world. You are asked to remember that you are part of it.

Stories of Initiation: The Boy and the Bowl

A young boy, eager and full of questions, once asked his grandmother, *"How do I become a Keeper of the Earth?"* His eyes were bright with determination, his chest lifted with pride, as though the very asking had already made him ready.

The grandmother, a woman whose hair shone like silver threads and whose eyes carried the weight of countless seasons, said nothing at first. Instead, she rose slowly, went to the shelf, and took down a simple clay bowl. She filled it with water until it nearly overflowed and placed it carefully in the boy's hands.

"Carry this," she said softly. *"Walk through the village and return to me when you are done. But do not spill a drop."*

The boy set out, his face tight with concentration. With each step, his eyes locked on the trembling water. He walked slowly, carefully, afraid that even the wind might disturb the bowl. Villagers greeted him, children called his name, birds soared overhead, but he did not look up. He kept his gaze fixed only on the bowl, guarding it like a treasure.

At last, he returned to his grandmother, chest swelling with pride. *"I have done it!"* he exclaimed. *"Not a single drop was lost."*

The grandmother smiled gently, her wrinkles folding like the lines of a map. *"Tell me then, child, what did you see on your walk? Did you notice the sky glowing with the colors of dawn? Did you see the old tree blooming for the first time this spring? Did you hear the sparrows calling to one another, or the stream laughing over stones?"*

The boy's face fell. He shook his head. *"No, Grandmother. I saw nothing but the bowl."*

Her eyes softened with both love and gravity. She laid her hand on his shoulder and said, *"Then you are not yet ready to be a Keeper. A true Keeper learns to carry the bowl carefully, yes, for the bowl is life, and to spill it carelessly is to wound the Earth. But a Keeper must also see the sky, greet the tree, hear the sparrow, feel the stream. A Keeper's task is not only to guard what is close, but to honor the whole."*

The boy's heart sank with shame, but she lifted his chin so his eyes met hers. *"Do not despair. To be a Keeper is not about perfection; it is about awareness. Try again tomorrow. Carry the bowl, but do not forget the world around you. Learn to walk with both care and wonder. For this is the path of the Keeper: steady hands, open eyes, and a heart wide enough to hold both the bowl and the beauty of the world."*

And so the boy understood that keeping was not guarding one thing at the expense of another. It was balanced. It was wholeness. It was the vow to protect life while never ceasing to marvel at it.

The Dream of Fire

One night, a woman burdened by fear and doubt fell into a restless sleep. Her days had been heavy with worry, and her nights no kinder, her mind crowded with shadows of what could go wrong. In her dream, she found herself standing before a wall of fire, towering, crackling, fierce. Its flames leaped upward like living creatures, their voices hissing and roaring.

Her first instinct was terror. Surely this was the end. Fire was destruction, the force that consumed forests, homes, and lives. She felt her body tremble, her breath catch in her throat. Every part of her screamed to turn and run.

But in the dream, her feet would not move. The fire seemed to call her, daring her to trust. And something deep within her, a spark she had long ignored, whispered, Go forward.

So, with trembling hands and racing heart, she stepped into the flames.

At first, she braced for pain. Yet the fire did not devour her. Instead, it wrapped around her like a cloak of light. The flames coursed over her skin, through her hair, into her chest, not burning, but illuminating. She felt her fear dissolve, her doubts fall away, her old wounds transformed into embers that lifted from her body like sparks, carried upward into the night sky.

She looked down at her hands, once clenched with anxiety, now glowing as if they themselves had become fire. The fear that had once defined her was gone. In its place was something steady, fierce, and beautiful: courage.

A voice rose from the heart of the flames, not loud, yet it filled the whole world: *"Now you know. You are Keeper of the Flame. This fire does not destroy, it transforms. Carry it without fear. Wherever you walk, let your courage be the light for others."*

The woman stepped out of the fire. Her body was untouched, yet she was not the same. She was radiant, her heart burning with strength, her eyes clear with purpose. From that day forward, she no longer shrank from challenges or let fear dictate her path. She carried herself with quiet power, not because she had no fear, but because she had learned what fire truly was: the element that purifies, reveals, and gives life.

And wherever she went, people felt something shift. In her presence, others stood taller, spoke braver, dreamed wider. For the flame she carried was not hers alone. It was the eternal fire, the light of the Keepers, that passed through her to all who dared to step into their own transformation.

Guided Meditation – Taking the Keeper's Vow

1. Prepare a simple altar: a stone, a bowl of water, a candle, and a feather or leaf.
2. Sit before it. Place your hands on your heart.
3. Whisper: *"Mother Earth, I hear you. I feel you. I remember."*
4. Speak your vow aloud, for example:
   "I vow to walk gently. I vow to love deeply. I vow to keep the circle unbroken."
5. Light the candle. See its flame as your vow.
6. Sit in silence, letting your body absorb the commitment.

Practices for Step 11

- **Keeper's Walk:** Walk outdoors in silence. With each step, whisper: *"Keeper's step, Keeper's breath, Keeper's heart."*

- **Keeper's Offering:** Leave a gift for Earth each week, a song, water, flowers, or prayer.
- **Keeper's Fire:** Light a candle daily, whispering: *"May this flame never go out within me."*
- **Keeper's Journal:** Write your vow in your own words. Read it daily.

Journaling Pages

- What does *"Keeper"* mean to you in your own language?
- What vow feels alive in your heart right now?
- What gifts or talents can you offer as a Keeper?
- How will you remind yourself of your vow when life grows heavy?

Poetic Closing

The vow is spoken, whispered from your heart to the heart of the Earth. The flame is lit, not only before you, but within you, burning steady and true. The circle is sealed, woven of ancestors and descendants, of dreamers and doers, of all who keep the memory alive.

You are Keeper now, Keeper of memory, that the wisdom of ages is never lost. Keeper of light, that even in darkness the fire will not go out. Keeper of Earth, tending soil, stone, water, and sky with reverence. Keeper of love, carrying compassion where the world has forgotten it.

Walk gently, for every step is prayer. Walk boldly, for courage is now your companion. Walk faithfully, for the circle walks beside you. The Earth breathes with you, the fire burns through you, the vow lives in you.

You are Keeper now. And the Earth, beloved child, is keeping you.

STEP 12:

THE PATH AHEAD

Invocation

River of tomorrow, light of becoming, breath of the unborn, song of the eternal, I walk into the future with courage, with reverence, with love.

The Threshold Beyond

The path of the Earth Keeper does not end with the vow. In truth, the vow is not a finish line but a doorway. It is the moment you step into a life of continual practice.

To walk as a Keeper is to live awake, not just in moments of ceremony or at sacred sites, but in the ordinary rhythm of your days. It is in the way you prepare food, the way you greet your neighbor, the way you place your feet on the ground each morning.

The Earth is calling not only for the healing of her forests, waters, and skies, but for the healing of human hearts. The future is not only ecological; it is relational. The Path Ahead is the weaving of both a vision where Gaia thrives and humanity thrives with her, where no separation remains between the healing of the planet and the healing of the soul.

Prophecies of Renewal

For generations, elders and visionaries across traditions have spoken of a time of great change. These prophecies are not warnings of inevitable doom, but invitations to step into possibility:

- **Hopi Prophecy:** A rainbow tribe will rise, people of all colors, nations, and walks of life, who will live in harmony and restore balance to the Earth.

- **Andean Prophecy:** The condor of the South (heart, intuition, spirit) and the eagle of the North (mind, reason, science) will fly together once more, uniting ancient wisdom and modern knowledge.
- **Revelation (Christian):** The New Jerusalem descends, not as a collapse, but as a renewal, where divine presence dwells with humanity and creation is restored.
- **Buddhist Vision of Maitreya:** The future Buddha comes not to rule, but to remind humanity of compassion, loving-kindness, and the eternal potential for awakening.
- **Māori Whakapapa:** When people remember their genealogy, that they are kin with rivers, mountains, stars, and all life, the Earth will flourish again.

Across traditions, the threads converge: the future is not an apocalypse to fear, but a transformation to be embodied. A healed Earth. A renewed humanity.

Sacred-Historical Pathways Forward

The way forward is not invented from nothing. It has always been walked. We are invited to re-enter practices that kept humanity in balance for millennia:

- **Pilgrimage Continues:** The journey is never finished. Sacred mountains, rivers, forests, and groves are teachers, visiting them renews our vow.
- **Seasonal Rituals:** Marking solstices, equinoxes, and harvests aligns human rhythm with cosmic cycles, reminding us of our place in the larger dance.
- **Community Circles:** Councils, sanghas, fire circles, and gatherings affirm that the path is not solitary but shared. We heal most deeply in community.
- **Keeper's Work:** Healing bodies, planting gardens, restoring rivers, teaching children, tending the sick, creating art, all of this is Keeper's work, each act a step along the sacred path.

Every gesture of reverence, no matter how small, becomes a thread in the excellent weaving of the future.

Science Echoes the Future

Even modern science, peering through its instruments, affirms what spirit has whispered all along: the Earth is alive, and humanity has the power to co-create renewal.

- **Regeneration:** Forests regrow, rivers cleanse, and coral reefs recover when humans stop exploiting and start restoring. Earth's resilience is astonishing when given space.
- **Collective Meditation:** Studies show that focused group intention measurably reduces violence and conflict in cities. Human consciousness shapes fields of reality.
- **Resonance and Frequency:** Research into sound, vibration, and energy medicine is rediscovering truths long known to shamans and mystics, that the universe itself is song.
- **Neuroplasticity of Humanity:** Just as individual brains rewire through new patterns, collective humanity evolves through new choices. We are shaping our destiny thought by thought, act by act.

Science confirms: the future is not fixed. We are not passengers but participants. The frequencies of Earth shift, and so do we.

The Spiritual Meaning

The Path Ahead is not about perfection. It is about participation, not about waiting for salvation, but about embodying renewal here and now.

To walk the Path Ahead means:

- To live every day in reverence, as if each step is a prayer.
- To act with love, especially in small, unnoticed ways, for these are the seeds of transformation.

- To carry hope when despair tempts, knowing that hope itself is medicine.
- To remember that the Earth walks with you, you are never alone.

You are an ancestor of the future. Every choice you make, every word you speak, every act you offer becomes a gift or burden to those who come after.

As Keeper, you do not only live for yourself. You live for the children of tomorrow, for the forests yet to grow, for the rivers yet to sing. You live as part of the eternal lineage of love and light.

And so the circle does not close. The vow does not end. The path continues, step by step, breath by breath, heart by heart, into the radiant future we are creating together.

Stories of the Future: The Child's Question

One evening, as the sun melted into gold and crimson behind the hills, a young girl sat beside her grandfather beneath an old cedar tree. She held a stone in her hand, turning it over curiously, as children often do, then looked up at the weathered lines on her grandfather's face.

"Grandfather," she asked softly, *"what will the Earth be like when I am old?"*

The old man grew quiet. He gazed at the horizon where sky met land, as though searching for the right words in the distance. The wind moved gently through the cedar branches, carrying the scent of resin and age. Finally, he placed his hand over the child's and spoke.

"That, little one, depends," he said. *"If you and others walk gently, she will blossom. Her rivers will sing, her forests will grow tall, her skies will shine clear. She will laugh with you, feed you, and hold you as a mother does. But if you forget her, if you take without gratitude, she will weep. Her waters will grow bitter, her soil tired,*

her breath heavy with smoke. And her tears will not fall from the sky alone; they will fall from the hearts of those who forgot her. "

The child listened, eyes wide and full of questions. *"But Grandfather,"* she whispered, *"what if others forget, even if I remember?"*

The elder smiled, though his eyes glistened with both sadness and hope. *"Then you, child, must remember even more strongly. For one who remembers can awaken another. One who loves can inspire love. The Earth does not ask for all to be perfect, only for some to keep the flame alive until others see the light again."*

He drew a circle in the soil with his finger and placed the stone the child had been holding in its center. *"You see, you are part of her story. Just as this stone rests in the circle of the Earth, so do you. What she becomes, you become too. Her health is your health. Her joy is your joy. Her wounds are your wounds. And when she heals, you will heal as well."*

The girl leaned against her grandfather's shoulder, the weight of his words settling into her heart. In the silence that followed, the Earth itself seemed to speak, the rustle of leaves, the call of a bird, the rhythm of her own heartbeat echoing the truth.

Years later, when the girl had grown, she would tell her own children the same lesson: that the Earth's future is not fixed, but written in the choices of every step, every breath, every act of care. She would tell them that to love the Earth is to love themselves, and to forget her is to lose themselves.

For in the question of the child and the answer of the elder, the eternal truth was spoken: humanity and Earth are one story, and it is still being written.

The Dream of Renewal

One night, a weary dreamer, troubled by the state of the world, lay down with a heavy heart. She had seen too many stories of destruction, forests burning, rivers poisoned, animals vanishing, and people divided. Her chest ached with the weight of despair, and she whispered into the dark, *"Is this all we are becoming?"*

That night, her sleep carried her into a vision.

She found herself walking across a desert, the sand hot beneath her feet. Yet instead of emptiness, she saw green shoots breaking through the cracked soil, flowers of colors she had never seen unfolded in great waves, carpeting the once-barren land. The desert was blooming, radiant with life.

She turned and saw the oceans. No longer silent, no longer stripped, they were alive with whales breaching joyfully, dolphins leaping in pods, coral reefs glowing like underwater cathedrals. The waters shimmered with light, carrying songs that seemed to rise not only from the creatures but from the ocean itself.

Then her vision shifted. She stood in the center of a city, but it was unlike any city she had ever known. Towers were clothed in vines, rooftops blossomed with gardens, fruit trees lined the streets, and children played in fountains of clean, clear water. People moved slowly, not rushing. They walked with reverence, touching leaves, greeting one another with kindness, pausing to sing with birds perched nearby. Every step felt like a prayer, every word like a blessing.

She listened and realized the world was alive with song. Not only the voices of humans, but the rivers, trees, winds, and stones, all singing together, weaving one melody. The song was familiar, like something she had always known but forgotten. It was harmony itself.

As she stood trembling in awe, a voice rose, not from outside her, but from within and around her all at once. It was vast, ancient, yet tender, like the voice of both mother and child.

"This is not fantasy," the voice said. *"This is a memory of the future. This is what waits for you, for all of you, when you walk with reverence, when you remember your belonging. The Earth is not dying; she is calling you to awaken. Walk toward this vision. Every choice, every prayer, every act of care brings it closer."*

Tears streamed down the dreamer's face. She fell to her knees, placing her hands upon the soil of that future Earth, feeling its strength and tenderness. She breathed it into her chest until her heart beat in rhythm with it.

When she awoke, the despair that had once weighed so heavily upon her was gone. In its place was a quiet certainty, a flame of hope that nothing could extinguish. She understood that the dream was not a gift meant only for her, it was a message for all.

From that day forward, she lived differently. She planted trees, walked gently, spoke with kindness, and carried water with gratitude. Whenever others spoke of despair, she shared her vision: deserts blooming, oceans alive, cities singing. And she told them, *"It is not a fantasy. It is a memory of the future. If we walk together, we will find it."*

And slowly, those who heard her began to believe.

Guided Meditation – Walking into the Future

1. Close your eyes. Place your feet firmly on the Earth.
2. Imagine standing at a wide river, the River of Tomorrow.
3. Step into it. Feel the current carry you forward, strong yet gentle.
4. On the far bank, see visions of a healed Earth, clear skies, thriving forests, joyful communities.
5. Whisper: *"I walk toward this vision. I walk as Keeper of the future."*

6. Rest in gratitude, then return with courage renewed.

Practices for Step 12

- **Future Letter:** Write a letter to your great-grandchildren (real or imagined). Share what you vow to do for Earth.
- **Vision Walk:** Take a walk outdoors while visualizing what a healed world looks like. Speak it aloud as you walk.
- **Keeper's Seed:** Plant a tree or garden as an offering to the future. Care for it as a symbol of the path ahead.
- **Circle of Hope:** Gather with others. Each person shares one vision for Earth's future. Seal it with prayer.

Journaling Pages

- What vision of a healed Earth lives in your heart? Describe it.
- What one daily practice can you commit to carrying forward?
- How do you wish to be remembered as an ancestor of the future?
- When you imagine Earth speaking through you, what does she say about tomorrow?

Poetic Closing

The path stretches forward, wide as the horizon, endless as the stars. The circle is unbroken, elders and children, ancestors and descendants, dreamers and keepers, all walking with you. The fire still burns, in the hearth of the Earth, in the rhythm of your heart, in the eternal flame that no shadow can extinguish.

You are the prayer of your ancestors, their whispered hopes, their sacrifices, their songs carried forward in your breath. You are the dream of your descendants, the yet-unborn who look to you, trusting you to leave them a world where love still blossoms. You are the heartbeat of Gaia in human form, a pulse of Earth's memory, a living thread in her great weaving.

So walk with courage, even when the road feels uncertain. Walk with love, even when the world forgets how. Walk awake, for your steps leave echoes in the soil and in the soul of those who come after.

The path ahead is endless, it will carry you beyond fear, beyond time, into the great unfolding. And yet it always begins here, in this breath, in this choice, in this moment. Step gently. Step boldly. Step with reverence.

For the Earth walks with you, the circle surrounds you, and the fire within you will never die.

PART II INTEGRATION: LIVING AS A KEEPER

A KEEPER'S YEAR

SEASONAL PRACTICES

The Earth moves in seasons, and so do we. To walk as a Keeper is to align your life with these rhythms, honoring the gifts of each cycle of the year. The wheel of the seasons is not only the story of the Earth, it is the story of your own soul. Each season is a teacher, each season a mirror.

Spring, Emergence & Planting

The world awakens. Buds break through the soil, rivers swell with snowmelt, birds return with their songs. Spring is the season of beginnings, of courage to bloom after the darkness of winter.

- **Practice:** Plant seeds with intention. As you place them into the earth, whisper: *"May this grow in harmony, may this life feed life."* This can be vegetables, herbs, flowers, or even symbolic seeds, stones or shells placed into soil with prayer.
- **Meditation:** Close your eyes and picture your own soul as a garden. What is sprouting? What new qualities, projects, or dreams are breaking through the soil of your being? See them as seedlings in your heart, tender yet resilient.
- **Journal Prompt:** *What new part of me is ready to bloom? What has been lying dormant, waiting for spring?*
- **Sacred Action:** Walk in nature and notice the first signs of growth, buds, shoots, blossoms. Greet them as kin, offering thanks for their courage to emerge.

Summer, Radiance & Celebration

The sun is at its height. Fields are green, rivers strong, life abundant. Summer teaches us to live in radiance, to shine without apology, to celebrate the fullness of being alive.

- **Practice:** Spend one day outside from sunrise to sunset. Honor the arc of the sun as it blesses the Earth. Let your body remember what it feels like to move with the light.
- **Meditation:** Sit in the sun with your face turned upward. Feel warmth infuse your body. Whisper: *"I shine with the sun. I radiate life."* Imagine yourself glowing with golden light, a beacon of joy and strength.
- **Journal Prompt:** What am I most grateful for in this season of abundance? How can I share my gifts freely, as the sun shares its light?
- **Sacred Action:** Create or join a celebration, a meal, dance, or gathering outdoors. Honor not only the abundance of Earth but also the abundance of community.

Autumn, Release & Harvest

Leaves turn, fields are gathered, nights grow cool. Autumn is both a feast and a farewell. It is the season of gratitude and letting go.

- **Practice:** Create a gratitude feast. Prepare food with reverence, perhaps using seasonal harvests, and share it with loved ones. Speak aloud what you are thankful for. Thank the Earth for her abundance.
- **Meditation:** Walk among falling leaves. Hold one in your hand. Whisper: *"I release with grace, as the tree releases its leaves. I trust that endings are beginnings."*
- **Journal Prompt:** What can I let go of now, so that new life may grow later? What harvest of wisdom or gratitude do I carry from this year?
- **Sacred Action:** Offer something back to the land, scatter seeds for birds, compost scraps, or leave an offering of cornmeal, flowers, or song.

Winter, Stillness & Renewal

The Earth rests. Seeds lie hidden, waters freeze, nights stretch long. Winter is the season of silence, of renewal in the dark, of remembering that stillness is fertile.

- **Practice:** Light a candle each night. Sit quietly before it. Let the flame remind you of the inner fire that never dies, even in the deepest dark.
- **Meditation:** Lie upon the Earth, even upon snow or frost if you are able, and feel her deep rest beneath you. Whisper: *"I enter the silence. I honor renewal."*
- **Journal Prompt:** What wisdom is found in my silence? What truths do I hear only when the world grows quiet?
- **Sacred Action:** Simplify your days. Reduce unnecessary noise and commitments. Let your body and spirit rest in rhythm with Earth's wintering.

30 DAYS OF LIVING AS A KEEPER

For those ready to walk daily with the Earth, here is a month of small yet profound practices. Each takes only minutes, but together they weave a new rhythm of belonging.

Week 1 – Listening

1. Walk barefoot for 5 minutes, feeling the soil.
2. Watch the sunrise in silence.
3. Sit with a stone. Place it in your palm. Listen.
4. Drink water slowly, as blessing. Whisper gratitude before each sip.
5. Place your hand on a tree and whisper thanks.
6. Write in your journal about a childhood memory of Earth.
7. Rest outdoors for 10 minutes, without agenda, simply be.

Week 2 – Connection

1. Draw your personal web of life, all beings you are connected to.
2. Feed the birds or animals near your home.
3. Share a smile with a stranger, an offering of human kindness.
4. Light a candle for your ancestors. Speak their names if you know them.
5. Offer clean water to the soil or plants.
6. Sing softly outdoors, letting your voice mingle with wind and leaves.
7. Journal: What threads connect me most deeply today?

Week 3 – Healing

1. Bathe with intention, imagine the water cleansing your spirit.
2. Sit in silence with your heart, feel its rhythm.
3. Offer gratitude before every meal, honoring land, farmer, and sun.
4. Release a burden, whisper it into river, wind, or fire.

5. Meditate with breath as prayer: inhale gratitude, exhale love.
6. Journal: How has Earth healed me?
7. Take a slow, mindful walk, each step a blessing.

Week 4 – Keeper's Vow

1. Write your own Earth Keeper vow.
2. Plant something, a seed, herb, or tree.
3. Share your vow aloud with a trusted friend.
4. Give a gift to the land, flowers, song, or prayer.
5. Spend 30 minutes in silence with Earth, listening.
6. Journal: How am I living as a Keeper today?
7. Hold a stone in meditation. Whisper: *"I am Keeper of the Earth."*
8. Walk beneath the stars. Whisper: *"I belong to the whole."*
9. Place your hands on your heart. Whisper: *"The path continues with me."*

KEEPER'S BLESSINGS & DAILY PRAYERS

Short invocations for morning, evening, or any sacred pause. Use them daily to align with Earth's rhythm.

Morning Blessing Mother Earth, I rise with you. Father Sky, I shine with you. Waters of life, flow through me. Fire of spirit, burn within me. This day I walk as Keeper, in reverence, in love, in truth.

Evening Blessing As the sun sets, I give thanks. For breath, for bread, for love, for life. I release my burdens into your keeping, and rest in your embrace. Keeper I was today, Keeper I shall be tomorrow.

Blessing for Water Sacred water, flow through me. Cleanse my heart, heal my body, renew my spirit. I honor you as life itself.

Blessing for Land Sacred soil, hold me steady. You are the body of my body, the ground of my being. May I walk gently upon you, as child upon the breast of Mother.

Blessing for Fire Flame of spirit, burn in me. Illuminate my mind, warm my heart, ignite my purpose. I carry you forward with courage.

Blessing for Air Breath of life, move through me. Teach me to speak with kindness, to listen with openness, to breathe in gratitude.

Poetic Closing of the Integration

The seasons turn, and with them, you turn. The days unfold, and with them, you unfold.

Each morning is not only a beginning but a gift placed in your hands, a flame newly kindled, a chance to breathe again with the Earth.

Each night is not only a return but a remembering, a resting back into the arms of the Mother, a surrender to the great rhythm that holds all things.

Keeper, your life itself is the ritual. It is not only in the temple or the grove, not only in prayer circles or sacred fires. It is in the simple act of rising with the sun, in the way you break bread, in the way you hold silence, in the way you speak to those you love, in the way you bow, even unseen, to the ground that carries your steps.

Your breath is not ordinary. Each inhale is a receiving of the world. Each exhale is a giving back. This endless exchange, you and tree, you and wind, you and ocean tide, is the most ancient prayer, the one that has always kept life alive.

Your steps are not mere motion. Every footfall is an offering to the soil. Every path you walk writes itself into the Earth. Do you know the power of this? The land remembers the rhythm of your walking, the way your body sings as it moves, the way your heart leaves echoes in the fields.

Your life is not random, but woven. You are thread in the great tapestry, light among countless lights, a voice in the endless choir. And whether you whisper or roar, whether you stumble or dance, your presence is part of the whole.

So walk on, not hurried, not afraid, but with reverence. Walk as though every stone is altar, every stream is oracle, every leaf is scripture, every breath is sacred song.

The path is endless, because it is not a road outside you, it is the way of being within you. You do not walk toward belonging; you have always belonged. You do not walk toward the sacred; you are the sacred in motion.

And when you grow weary, when the night feels too long, remember: you do not walk alone. The ancestors walk with you. The children yet unborn walk with you. The rivers, the mountains, the winds, all keep pace beside you.

The Earth walks with you, not as guide above you, not as burden beneath you, but as mother, as mirror, as companion.

Keeper, you are not simply living life. You are weaving prayer. You are carrying flame. You are turning the wheel of seasons with every breath.

So let your days be blessings, your nights be peace, your footsteps be offerings, your voice be truth, your hands be healing, your heart be flame.

For the path stretches beyond horizon, yet it is here, under your feet. It begins again each morning. It continues through every dusk. It is endless, eternal, whole.

And you, you are Keeper of it all.

Walk on. The Earth walks with you.

Walking the Vow: What We Can Do for the Earth (and Ourselves)

The vow of the Earth Keeper is not only whispered in prayer, not only felt in meditation, not only lit in ritual fires. It must also be walked, lived, and embodied in the choices we make every single day.

To walk the vow is to remember that our lives are not separate from Earth's life. Every action we take for her health becomes a gift to our own bodies, minds, and spirits. Every time we heal her wounds, we ease our own. Every time we honor her rhythms, we return ourselves to balance.

The path of the Keeper is personal. It belongs to each of us. It is not abstract, it is what you eat, how you move, what you breathe, what you build, and how you love. It is how you live in this body, on this soil, within this miracle we call Earth.

1. Restore the Soil, Restore Your Food

- **For Earth:** Compost scraps instead of throwing them away. Garden without chemicals. Support local farmers who care for the land. Protect topsoil as though it were gold, because it is: it holds the seed of life itself.
- **For You:** When you do this, you eat food that is alive with nutrients. Your body grows stronger, your immune system steadier, and your connection to life deepens. You taste food with reverence because you know where it came from.

Soil is memory. Soil is womb. To restore soil is to restore the ground of your being.

2. Protect the Waters, Heal Your Body

- **For Earth:** Say no to plastic bottles, microbeads, and toxic runoff. Conserve fresh water as though it were sacred wine. Protect rivers and oceans as though they were your veins.
- **For You:** When you honor the waters, you drink more purely. Your body hydrates, your mind clears, your emotions settle. You feel the life-giving flow of vitality.

Water is blood. Water is clarity. When you heal the waters, your own blood remembers how to flow freely.

3. Plant Trees, Breathe Freely

- **For Earth:** Trees absorb carbon, shade the soil, and shelter countless lives. Each sapling planted is a promise of future generations breathing freely.
- **For You:** Walk among trees and your stress dissolves. Sit beneath them and your lungs open. You breathe not just oxygen but peace, calm, and beauty.

Trees are lungs. Trees are memory. When you plant one, you are planting breath for your grandchildren.

4. Walk and Cycle More, Live Longer

- **For Earth:** Each step you take instead of driving reduces pollution. Each mile walked or cycled is one less weight pressing on Gaia's body.
- **For You:** Walking restores the heart. Cycling strengthens the body. Moving through the world at the pace of your breath connects you to the land again.

Movement is medicine. To walk upon the Earth is to love her with your body.

5. Reduce Waste, Simplify Your Life

- **For Earth:** Less garbage in landfills. Less plastic in the sea. Less energy wasted in factories.
- **For You:** Less clutter in your home. Less chaos in your mind. Less craving for what you don't truly need. Gratitude grows where excess falls away.

Simplicity is freedom. Every act of reduction makes room for joy.

6. Support Renewable Energy, Lighten Your Load

- **For Earth:** Choose solar, wind, or clean energy when you can. Every watt drawn from the sun is one less wound torn from her body.
- **For You:** Clean air to breathe. Lighter conscience. Alignment between your values and your actions.

Energy is choice. When you choose renewal, you align your life with the rising song of the future.

7. Honor Animals, Free Your Spirit

- **For Earth:** Protect habitats. Buy with care. Eat with compassion. Every animal saved is another thread in the tapestry of life unbroken.
- **For You:** Kindness feeds your spirit. Compassion lightens your body. Whether you eat differently, shop differently, or simply pause to bless the animals around you, your spirit grows wider.

Animals are kin. To honor them is to honor the circle of life itself.

8. Join Circles of Action, Find Your Belonging

- **For Earth:** Join with others: community gardens, river cleanups, tree plantings, prayer circles. Healing grows faster when it is shared.
- **For You:** You are not alone. To walk with others is to rediscover joy, strength, and purpose. The circle nurtures your gifts and multiplies their power.

Community is healing. When we gather, Earth heals through our unity.

The Keeper's Truth

Every act of care, no matter how small, is both ecological and spiritual. Every choice you make ripples outward: into your body, into your family, into your community, into the Earth herself.

When you compost, the soil sings. When you plant, the trees breathe. When you conserve water, rivers bless you. When you simplify your life, your spirit lightens. When you walk gently, Gaia feels you.

To heal her is to heal yourself. To heal yourself is to heal her.

This is the great reciprocity, the circle of love unbroken. This is the vow you carry. This is the life of the Earth Keeper.

Journaling Prompts

- Which of these actions feels most alive for me right now?
- What one change can I commit to this month?
- How can I make my daily choices reflect my Keeper's vow?
- What kind of ancestor do I want to be remembered as?

Poetic Closing – The Keeper's Prayer

- The Earth heals, and in her healing, your own wounds soften. The Earth breathes, and in her breath, your lungs remember their song. The Earth thrives, and in her thriving, your spirit finds renewal.
- Keeper, do you see? Every choice you make is not small, it is a prayer spoken in the language of soil and sky. When you drink water with reverence, you are praying. When you walk gently upon the ground, you are praying. When you choose kindness in what you eat, what you buy, and how you speak, you are weaving prayers into the fabric of the world.
- The Earth does not ask for perfection. She asks for presence. She asks that you remember her when you rise in the morning and when you lie down at night. She asks that your love be lived, not only spoken.
- For as you care for her, she carries you. As you honor her, she remembers you. As you live in harmony, she multiplies that harmony back to you.
- Keeper, walk gently, for your steps are offerings. Speak truthfully, for your words are seeds. Choose wisely, for your choices ripple like rivers into tomorrow.
- The Earth heals, and you heal with her. The circle is whole, the vow alive. Your life is prayer. Live it well.

KEEPER'S ACTION GUIDE

1. RESTORE THE SOIL, RESTORE YOUR FOOD

The Wisdom of Earth

Soil is not *"dirt."* Soil is alive. It is a vast, hidden community beneath our feet, billions of fungi, bacteria, insects, and roots engaged in endless exchange. A single teaspoon of healthy soil holds more life than there are humans on Earth. This unseen world is the foundation of all nourishment: it feeds the plants that feed the animals that feed us.

- Our ancestors knew this intimately. They prayed before planting, sang songs while harvesting, and gave offerings back to the ground that sustained them. They did not see soil as resource alone, but as living kin.
- The Inca carved terraces along mountainsides to protect soil from erosion, capturing water and nutrients so food would flourish for generations.
- The Maya practiced the milpa cycle, planting maize, beans, and squash together. Each plant gave and took, restoring the soil in harmony.
- The Celts poured milk and honey into furrows as libations, feeding the spirit of the land.

In contrast, much of modern agriculture forgets this wisdom. Heavy machinery compacts the ground, chemicals sterilize its life, and monocultures strip its fertility. But we can remember. When we restore soil, we are not only reviving the Earth, we are restoring ourselves. For what the soil holds, our bodies will one day eat, absorb, and become.

Science Confirms the Wisdom

- **Soil Microbiome & Gut Health:** Studies reveal that the diversity of microbes in soil directly mirrors the diversity in our own gut. Healthy soil creates nutrient-rich food, which fosters a healthier microbiome, improving immunity, mood, and longevity.
- **Regenerative Agriculture:** Practices like cover crops, no-till planting, and composting replenish carbon, restore fertility, and heal the land while reducing climate impact.
- **Earthing and Mental Health:** Contact with soil has been shown to trigger serotonin release. Mycobacterium vaccae, a soil microbe, is linked to reduced anxiety and depression. In other words, touching soil literally heals the mind.

The lesson is simple: when soil thrives, we thrive.

Spiritual Practice, Returning to the Soil

- Go to a garden, park, or natural place. With reverence, take a small pinch of soil in your palm. Whisper: *"Mother, I honor your body."*
- Smell it, feel its texture, imagine the invisible life teeming within. See how what looks small is in truth vast and infinite.
- Return it gently, or sprinkle it around a plant as blessing.
- This practice reconnects you not only to Earth, but also to your own body, which is born of soil and one day will return to it.

Practical Actions

- Begin a compost pile, return food scraps back to the soil.
- Grow one edible plant, on a balcony, in a pot, or in a yard. Witness life sprout from Earth's generosity.
- Support farmers who use organic or regenerative methods.
- Avoid pesticides and herbicides that kill soil's living network.

Keeper's Reflection

When I care for soil, I am caring for more than land. I am tending the health of my children, my community, and myself. Soil is not the ground beneath my feet, it is the memory of my ancestors, the nourishment of the present, and the promise of the future.

Journal Prompts:

- Recall a childhood moment of playing in the dirt or planting something. What did you feel?
- How can I restore the soil in my own life, literally through gardening, or symbolically by tending to neglected parts of myself?
- What food or plant could I begin growing as an act of devotion to the Earth?

2. PROTECT THE WATERS, HEAL YOUR BODY

The Wisdom of Water

Water is life. It is the first sound we hear in the womb, the element that carried our ancestors across oceans, the pulse that still flows through rivers and rain. Without water, there is no breath, no song, no future.

- Ancient peoples always honored water as sacred. They knew rivers, lakes, and springs as living beings, not resources to be drained.
- Egyptians honored the Nile as divine, its floods renewing the land each year.
- Hindus still bathe in the Ganges for purification, believing its waters wash karma as well as body.
- Celtic peoples tied ribbons to holy wells, leaving prayers to the spirit of the spring.
- West Africans sing to Oshun, goddess of rivers, and Mami Wata, spirit of seas, invoking beauty, fertility, and healing.

To protect the waters is to protect ourselves. Our blood mirrors the oceans in its salt balance. Our bodies are rivers clothed in skin. To pollute or bless water outside is to pollute or bless it within.

Science Confirms the Wisdom

- **Hydration & Health:** Clean water regulates temperature, aids digestion, carries nutrients, and sharpens the mind. Without it, the body falters.
- **Pollution & Disease:** Water contaminated with chemicals, plastics, or pathogens directly damages human health, from cancers to neurological issues.

- **Microplastics:** Fragments of plastic now flow in human bloodstreams, a sobering reminder that what we pour into rivers and seas inevitably returns to us.
- **Water Cycle Unity:** The water you drink today may once have flowed as rain over mountains, or as part of ancient seas that birthed life. You are drinking history, memory, and eternity in a single glass.

Science confirms what ancestors always felt: we are not separate from the waters, we are them.

Spiritual Practice, Blessing the Waters

- Pour a clear glass of water. Hold it in your hands. Whisper: *"Sacred water, I honor you. Flow pure, flow free."*
- Drink slowly, imagining clarity filling your body.
- Or, pour it outside as an offering, blessing soil, plants, or stones.
- Simple acts of reverence turn ordinary hydration into communion.

Practical Actions

- Reduce or eliminate single-use plastics that choke rivers and seas.
- Use natural cleaning products and avoid pesticides that poison water tables.
- Conserve water, take shorter showers, fix leaks, and honor its preciousness.
- Support groups protecting rivers, wetlands, and oceans.

Keeper's Reflection

When I bless the water, I do not bless something outside myself, I bless my very being. The glass I lift to my lips, the river that winds through the valley, the rain that falls upon the fields, all of these become my blood, my cells, my breath. What flows through streams flows through me. What falls from the sky finds its way into the rhythm of my heart.

When I pollute the water, I do not harm a distant sea or a hidden spring alone, I wound myself, my children, and the generations yet to come. The toxins poured into rivers will one day pass through human veins. The plastics that choke the ocean find their way into the marrow of our bones. The water remembers, and because I am water, I too remember.

My blood is the river. My body is the sea. My tears are the rains that fall, and my breath is mist rising from the waters at dawn. To honor the rivers is to honor my veins. To heal the oceans is to heal my spirit. To keep the springs pure is to keep my soul clear.

Every sip is communion. Every drop is prayer. Every choice is reflection of whether I live in harmony or in harm. To care for the waters is not only an act of environmental duty, it is to revere the temple of life, the holy current that flows both within me and around me, binding me to all that lives.

Journal Prompts:

- Recall a memory of water that felt holy, swimming, bathing, or drinking when deeply thirsty. What did it teach you?
- How do I honor the waters within my body?
- What is one daily change I can make to keep the waters clean for myself, my community, and future generations?

3. PLANT TREES, BREATHE FREELY

The Wisdom of Trees

Trees are the standing people. They root deep in the Earth, stretch upward toward the heavens, and breathe with us in a sacred exchange, exhaling oxygen for us, inhaling the carbon we release. They are bridges between soil and sky, silence and song, Earth and spirit.

Ancient peoples always revered trees:

- Druids held oaks as sacred temples, where wisdom was received.
- Buddha attained enlightenment beneath the Bodhi tree.
- Norse mythology speaks of Yggdrasil, the World Tree, connecting all realms.
- Native American traditions call trees *"our relatives,"* gathering medicine and teachings from them.

To plant and protect trees is not just an ecological act, it is a spiritual act. When you care for trees, you strengthen the lungs of the Earth and your own.

Science Confirms the Wisdom

- **Oxygen Exchange:** One mature tree can provide oxygen for two people every day.
- **Carbon Capture:** Forests absorb billions of tons of carbon annually, slowing climate change.
- **Cooling & Shelter:** Trees reduce heat in cities, shelter wildlife, and prevent erosion.
- **Mental Health:** Walking among trees reduces stress, lowers blood pressure, and restores focus.

Spiritual Practice, Breathing with a Tree

- Sit beneath a tree. Place your hand on its bark.
- Inhale deeply, imagining the oxygen it offers you.
- Exhale slowly, imagining the tree receiving your carbon dioxide.
- Whisper: *"We breathe as one."*

Practical Actions

- Plant a tree in your yard, neighborhood, or through reforestation projects.
- Protect forests by supporting sustainable wood and paper use.
- Volunteer with local tree-planting groups.
- Take children to plant trees, passing the vow forward.

Keeper's Reflection

When I plant a tree, I plant hope. When I breathe, I breathe with trees. Their roots steady me, their branches lift me, their breath sustains me. To honor trees is to honor life itself.

Journaling Prompts

- Recall a tree that felt special to you. What did it teach you?
- How does planting or protecting trees reflect your own inner growth?
- What vow would you like to whisper to a tree you plant?

4. WALK AND CYCLE MORE, LIVE LONGER

The Wisdom of Movement

Our ancestors walked everywhere. They followed rivers, crossed mountains, and carried the rhythm of the Earth in their steps. To move on foot or by simple wheels is to return to the body's natural pace, slow enough to notice, steady enough to endure, close enough to belong.

- Indigenous peoples walked trails that became trade routes, songlines, and pilgrimage paths.
- Buddhist monks practice kinhin, walking meditation, with each step a prayer.
- Muslims walk in pilgrimage around the Kaaba, circling in devotion.
- Christians once walked long distances to holy shrines, carrying offerings and prayers.

Walking and cycling are not just transport. They are pilgrimage, medicine, and communion with Earth.

Science Confirms the Wisdom

- **Longevity:** Regular walking and cycling reduce risk of heart disease, diabetes, and stroke.
- **Mental Health:** Gentle movement outdoors lowers stress, anxiety, and depression.
- **Creativity:** Studies show walking boosts problem-solving and inspiration.
- **Ecology:** Walking or cycling instead of driving lowers pollution and carbon output, protecting the very air we breathe.

Each step heals the body. Each mile heals the Earth.

Spiritual Practice, The Pilgrim's Step

- Choose a short path outdoors.
- With each inhale, whisper inwardly: *"Here."*
- With each exhale, whisper: *"Now."*
- Walk slowly, feeling the Earth beneath your feet.
- Let every step become a prayer of gratitude.

Practical Actions

- Walk or bike for short errands instead of driving.
- Begin or end your day with a 10-minute walk in nature.
- Encourage community bike paths, greenways, and walking trails.
- Use walking as reflection time, cycling as joyful release.

Keeper's Reflection

When I walk, I return to the rhythm that is older than memory, the steady beat of foot upon soil, echoing the heartbeat of the Earth beneath me. Each step carries me closer to presence, to the pulse of life that once guided our ancestors across plains, valleys, and forests. My soles press against her body, and she responds with strength rising into my bones. I am reminded that I do not move alone; I move in harmony with every creature who has ever walked this path before me.

When I cycle, I feel the wind rushing past, not as emptiness but as the breath of spirit itself. The air lifts me, cools me, carries me forward. In its currents I hear whispers of freedom, whispers of renewal. My breath joins with the wind, and suddenly I am not just riding through the world, I am carried within it, part of its invisible exhale.

With every movement, my body grows stronger, more resilient, more alive. My muscles remember what it means to belong, to be both rooted and free. Yet this strength is not mine alone, it is shared with the Earth. As I choose to walk instead of drive, to cycle instead of consume, the Earth breathes lighter. The air clears. The soil sighs in relief. The rivers sparkle with renewed vitality. My strength becomes her strength, my choices her healing.

Movement is prayer. It is the unspoken hymn of body and Earth remembering one another. Each step, each turn of the wheel, is an offering, not of words, but of action; not of ritual alone, but of life lived in reverence. In these simple acts, I carry no temple but the world itself, no altar but the path beneath my feet, no sacred song but the rhythm of my own heartbeat moving in time with Gaia.

And so, I walk, I cycle, I breathe, I move, not only for myself, but for the living Earth. For every step is a vow, every breath an offering, every journey a prayer of belonging.

Journaling Prompts

- Recall a time when walking cleared your mind or lifted your spirit. What did you notice?
- How could you shift one daily routine to include walking or cycling?
- If your footsteps left blessings behind, what would you want to gift the Earth with each step?

5. REDUCE WASTE, SIMPLIFY YOUR LIFE

The Wisdom of Simplicity

For most of human history, nothing was wasted. Bones became tools, cloth was patched and repatched, vessels were repaired and passed down. Everything was honored for the life it carried.

Waste is a modern wound, a forgetting of reverence. To reduce waste is not only about ecology; it is about remembering the sacredness of matter, of life. When we live simply, we live closer to truth.

Ancient cultures taught this naturally:

- Native American traditions used every part of the animal, giving thanks before and after. Waste was considered dishonor to the spirit of the creature.
- Japanese Shinto and Zen practices honor simplicity and minimalism, beauty in what is necessary, reverence in the uncluttered.
- Medieval monastics lived by vows of poverty, cherishing each item as sacred gift, never excess.
- Indigenous Andean peoples wove clothing to last generations, each thread a prayer, each garment an inheritance.

To live simply is to live free, free from the burden of excess, free from the lie that more equals better, free to see the beauty in enough.

Science Confirms the Wisdom

- **Planetary Impact:** Landfills release methane, a greenhouse gas far more potent than CO_2. Plastics break down into microplastics that now infiltrate oceans, soil, and even our own bloodstreams.

- **Health Effects:** Exposure to toxins from plastics, packaging, and waste products increases risk of illness, while reducing waste limits these dangers.
- **Psychological Health:** Studies show clutter raises cortisol (stress hormone), while simplification and tidiness promote peace of mind.
- **Circular Economy:** Research demonstrates that reusing, repairing, and recycling saves resources, energy, and money, benefitting both Earth and human communities.

Science now proves what wisdom keepers always knew: respect what you use, waste as little as possible, and life will flourish.

Spiritual Practice, The Ritual of Release

- Gather three items in your home you no longer need but that are still useful.
- Hold each one, whispering: *"Thank you for your service."*
- Give them away, to a person, a shelter, or a donation center.
- Imagine the energy of these objects continuing their journey, carrying blessing forward.
- This practice reminds us that letting go is not loss, it is flow.

Practical Actions

- **Refuse:** Say no to items you do not need, free trinkets, excess packaging, plastic bags.
- **Reduce:** Buy less, choose quality that lasts longer.
- **Reuse:** Repair what can be fixed; repurpose what can be given new life.
- **Recycle:** Sort with care, but remember recycling comes after refusing and reducing.
- **Compost:** Food scraps and natural matter return to soil instead of landfill.

Keeper's Reflection

Every item I touch carries a story. The cup in my hand was once clay in the Earth, hardened by fire and shaped by human care. The food on my plate was once seed and soil, tended by sun, rain, and countless unseen creatures who gave their lives so that I might be nourished. Even the simplest object carries the fingerprints of the cosmos: minerals born in stars, forests grown over centuries, rivers that flowed long before my time.

Nothing I hold is separate from the web of life. Every thread leads back to the Earth, to ancestors who discovered, harvested, or crafted, to human hands that labored, to energies drawn from the sun itself. To live without awareness of this is to walk blind, to mistake abundance for entitlement.

When I waste, I dishonor all of these. I dishonor the tree felled for paper, the waters drawn to grow food, the labor of those who toiled to bring it into being. Waste is not only the discarding of material things, it is the forgetting of relationship, the severing of gratitude.

When I choose to simplify, to take only what I need, I honor the chain of life. I honor the hands of the farmer, the breath of the forest, the gift of the Earth. I honor the truth that life is sustained not by endless consumption, but by reverence and balance. In simplicity, I discover richness: the taste of food is sweeter, the use of objects more meaningful, the gratitude for life more profound.

To reduce waste is not deprivation. It is liberation. It is the freedom of no longer being bound by endless wanting, of no longer drowning in what does not matter. It is the humility of recognizing that I am a guest here on Earth, not her master. It is the gratitude of knowing that every resource shared is a blessing, and every act of restraint is a prayer for generations yet to come.

Each choice I make, to reuse, to mend, to refuse what I do not need, becomes an act of devotion. Each step toward simplicity becomes a step toward harmony. And in this way, my life becomes lighter, my heart becomes freer, and my spirit becomes aligned with the great rhythm of giving and receiving that sustains all creation.

Stories of Simplicity - The Monk's Bowl

A Zen monk was once known throughout his village for carrying only a single bowl. Wherever he went, whether walking through the forest, sitting in meditation, or sharing a meal with others, that one bowl was always with him. It was chipped at the rim, smoothed by years of use, and polished by countless washings in river water.

One day, a visitor asked him with curiosity, *"Why do you own so little? Would you not be more comfortable with another bowl, perhaps a spare for guests or one more finely made?"*

The monk smiled gently, lifting the bowl into the light. *"How many mouths do I have?"* he asked. *"One. One bowl is enough."*

For him, this bowl was not merely an object. It was teacher and mirror. It reminded him of sufficiency, that his needs were few and already met. It reminded him of gratitude, for every meal placed within it came not from wealth but from the generosity of the Earth and the kindness of others. It reminded him of presence, for when he ate, he ate simply, no feast to distract him, no excess to dull his senses.

Over time, the villagers began to see the wisdom in the monk's way. They noticed how he savored each grain of rice as though it were precious, how he bowed in reverence before and after every meal, how his bowl, though simple, carried the fullness of life. He did not hunger for what he did not have; instead, he overflowed with peace for what he did.

His life was not filled with possessions, but with presence. Each moment became a banquet. Each breath, each sip of water, each bite of food was honored as sacred.

The lesson of the monk's bowl is not about poverty, nor is it about austerity. It is about freedom. To hold one bowl and call it enough is to remember that abundance is not measured by how much we own, but by how deeply we are able to receive the gifts already before us.

In this way, the monk's bowl becomes a symbol for all of us. What is our *"one bowl"*? What is truly enough for our bodies, our hearts, our lives? If we can answer honestly, and live simply with that answer, we too may discover the fullness that arises not from accumulation, but from presence.

The Woman Who Released

There was once a modern woman who lived surrounded by things. Her closets overflowed with clothes she rarely wore. Her shelves sagged beneath trinkets and souvenirs she hardly noticed. Her drawers were filled with objects she kept *"just in case,"* though she could not remember the last time she had used them.

At first, she believed these possessions brought comfort, that they were evidence of a full life. But over time, she began to feel suffocated. The clutter around her seemed to mirror the clutter within her mind, constant noise, endless choices, a weight pressing down upon her spirit. She longed for space, for air, for a sense of freedom she could not find among her crowded belongings.

One day, in a moment of clarity, she decided to let go. Slowly at first, she began to give things away, a shirt here, a box of books there. Each time she released something, she felt lighter, as if a stone had been lifted from her chest. The rooms in her home began to breathe again, and so did she.

What surprised her most was not only the physical space that opened, but the emotional and spiritual space. Without piles of objects demanding her attention, she found herself calmer, more present. She began to notice the way sunlight fell across an empty floor, how peaceful it felt to sit in a room uncluttered, how easy it was to create when her surroundings were simple.

The more she released, the more she discovered what truly mattered. Relationships deepened. Her creativity flourished. She found time to walk in nature, to write, to listen to her own heart. She laughed more easily, loved more fully, and lived with greater joy.

Later, when asked about her transformation, she said, *"The less I owned, the more space I had, not just in my home, but in my soul. I made room to breathe, to create, to love. I thought I was giving things up, but really, I was receiving my life back."*

Her story is a reminder for us all: possessions can weigh down the spirit when they are more than we need. To release is not to lose, but to gain, freedom, clarity, and the profound gift of presence.

Journaling Prompts

- What possessions in my life weigh me down instead of lift me up?
- How do I feel when I simplify, calmer, freer, clearer?
- What is one daily habit I can change to reduce waste?
- If I lived with only what I truly needed, what would my life look like?

A Ritual for the Keeper's Home

- Once each season, walk through your home.
- For each object, ask: *"Do I use this? Does it bring joy? Does it serve life?"*
- Keep what aligns. Release what does not.
- Offer gratitude for both keeping and releasing.

Poetic Closing

The Earth gives without measure. She offers soil rich with memory, rivers that quench all thirst, forests that breathe life into the sky, and fire that warms and renews. Every grain of rice, every drop of rain, every ray of sunlight upon my face is her blessing, freely poured.

I receive with open hands. I bow to the mystery of seed becoming fruit, of water becoming blood, of stone becoming shelter. I recognize that nothing I touch is mine alone, it is part of the endless cycle of giving and receiving that sustains all beings.

I honor each gift. No breath is taken for granted, no meal unblessed, no moment unnoticed. Even the smallest offering, a fallen leaf, a sip of water, a single step upon the soil, is holy. And so I walk gently, speak softly, live gratefully.

I waste nothing. For to waste is to forget, and to forget is to wound the chain of life. I remember that each item I hold carries the labor of Earth, of ancestors, of unseen hands and hidden lives. To discard carelessly is to dishonor them. To live mindfully is to restore them.

I choose simplicity. Not as denial, but as freedom. Not as emptiness, but as fullness. For in simplicity, I discover space to breathe, room to love, and time to remember. And in my simplicity, others may simply live, the children yet unborn, the forests yet uncut, the rivers yet unpolluted.

Keeper, your life is already enough. Not because of what you own, but because of how you live. Not because of how much you carry, but because of how deeply you care. The Earth does not ask for riches or grandeur, she asks for presence, for reverence, for love.

And so I vow: To live as blessing, not burden. To walk as prayer, not demand. To remember that my choices are seeds, planted in the soil of tomorrow. May they bloom as gratitude, as beauty, as life.

6. SUPPORT RENEWABLE ENERGY, LIGHTEN YOUR LOAD

The Wisdom of Light

From the beginning of time, humanity has lived by the rhythms of natural energy. The rising and setting sun was the first clock, the first teacher of cycles. Fire gave warmth and protection, wind carried ships across oceans, and rivers turned the earliest wheels of industry. These energies were not *"resources"* in the modern sense, they were gifts, freely given, endlessly renewed, woven into the cycles of life itself.

It is only in recent centuries that humans turned away from these eternal sources, digging deep into the Earth to extract fuels that burn fast, foul the air, and heat the planet beyond balance. These sources seemed powerful, but they came with a cost, smog-filled skies, poisoned rivers, and a climate now trembling under their weight.

To return to renewable energy is not merely innovation; it is remembrance. It is the reawakening of an ancient truth: that the sun, the wind, the waters, and the fire are sacred companions, not commodities. It is a choice to live in reverence rather than exploitation, to walk lightly rather than heavily, to align with the eternal flow instead of the extractive hunger of the modern age.

Throughout cultures and ages, natural energy was honored as divine:

- Egyptians worshiped Ra, the radiant sun god, seeing in him the giver of life and light.
- Greeks prayed to Helios, the charioteer of the sun, and to Aeolus, the keeper of winds.
- Indigenous peoples across the Earth honored fire, wind, and water as living beings, spirits that sustain life and guide balance.
- Hindu traditions still honor Agni, the fire god, through daily offerings of flame, acknowledging that energy itself is holy.

Energy is not only physical. It is spiritual. To draw it respectfully is to live in alignment with creation's song.

Science Confirms the Wisdom

Modern science now echoes what ancient people knew in their bones, that clean energy is life-giving:

- **Renewable Energy Growth:** Solar and wind are the fastest-growing energy sources in the world, offering hope that humanity can shift away from destructive fuels.
- **Air Quality:** Clean energy drastically reduces pollution, preventing millions of premature deaths from respiratory disease each year.
- **Climate Balance:** Renewable power cuts carbon emissions, slowing the advance of climate chaos and giving ecosystems space to heal.
- **Economic Renewal:** Studies show that renewable energy creates more jobs per dollar invested than fossil fuels, bringing not just sustainability, but prosperity to communities.

The sun does not send a bill. The wind does not run dry. The river flows long after we are gone. The more we align with these endless gifts, the lighter Earth's burden becomes, and the lighter our own hearts and lives become as well.

Spiritual Practice, The Candle of the Sun

- At dawn or dusk, light a simple candle. Hold it gently and whisper: *"As this flame is small, so are my needs. As the sun is vast, so are its gifts."*
- Sit in silence for a few moments, feeling the warmth of the flame on your skin. Imagine the great sunlight flowing through you, illuminating your heart, energizing your spirit.

- Carry that sense of gratitude into your day, remembering that energy is not something to be consumed thoughtlessly, but to be honored as sacred exchange.

Practical Actions

- If possible, choose renewable energy options from your utility provider, or support community solar and wind projects.
- Install solar panels, or explore ways to support renewable co-ops if direct installation isn't possible.
- Reduce reliance on fossil fuels by insulating your home, using energy-efficient appliances, and being mindful of electricity use.
- Support leaders, organizations, and policies that invest in renewable energy infrastructure, ensuring the future belongs to clean light rather than dirty smoke.
- Begin small: turn off unnecessary lights, unplug unused electronics, honor each watt of energy as if it were flame from a sacred fire.

Keeper's Reflection

When I walk in the sunlight, I feel the ancient fire upon my skin. When I hear the wind in the trees, I feel its song moving through me. These are not luxuries, they are life. When I live in alignment with renewable energy, I honor the oldest covenant between humanity and the Earth: take only what is given, give back only what can be renewed.

Each time I choose light over shadow, clean energy over destructive fuel, I lighten the Earth's burden. And I lighten my own.

Journaling Prompts

- How do I already receive energy from natural cycles (sunlight, wind, water)?

- What is one change I can make to shift toward renewable energy in my home or habits?
- How would my life feel if all my energy use was in harmony with Earth?

Poetic Closing

The sun rises, not because we command it, but because it is faithful to the rhythm of life. It pours its golden warmth across the Earth, reminding us that light is never truly lost, only waiting to be born again.

The wind blows, invisible yet undeniable. It carries seeds across valleys, songs across oceans, and whispers of spirit into our lungs. Each breath we take is a gift of the wind, a reminder that we are sustained by what cannot be seen.

The river flows, never clinging, never still for long. It carves valleys, nourishes fields, and carries stories from mountain to sea. Its waters touch every corner of the Earth, just as they touch every cell of our bodies. The river teaches us how to move, how to release, how to begin again.

Endless gifts, given freely without demand for repayment. Endless light, shining upon all equally, upon saint and sinner, upon forest and stone, upon child yet unborn.

To live as a Keeper is to notice these gifts, to bow in gratitude, to walk with humility, and to remember that we too are meant to be givers. For as the sun rises, so may our hearts rise in compassion. As the wind blows, so may our voices carry truth and kindness. As the river flows, so may our lives move in generosity and grace.

The Earth does not ask us to be perfect. She asks us only to remember: that her gifts are endless, and that we are part of their endless flow.

Keeper, walk lightly, your power is the Earth's power.

7. HONOR ANIMALS, FREE YOUR SPIRIT

The Wisdom of Kinship

From the first fire circles to the present day, animals have been our companions, teachers, and guides. They have fed us, clothed us, carried us across continents, and protected us from danger. Yet beyond their utility, they have offered something greater, wisdom written in fur, feather, scale, and song.

To honor animals is to remember kinship. They are not *"resources,"* nor shadows beneath us, they are our relatives in the great family of life. Their eyes mirror our fears and hopes. Their voices echo the same pulse of Earth that beats within us.

Across the world, traditions remind us of this sacred bond:

- Indigenous peoples speak of *"all my relations,"* acknowledging deer, eagle, salmon, wolf, and bear as family within the web of life.
- Ancient Egyptians revered Bastet the cat, guardian of home and joy; Anubis the jackal, protector of thresholds; and Horus the falcon, symbol of vision.
- Hindu traditions honor sacred cows as mothers of nourishment, elephants as bearers of wisdom in the form of Ganesha, and monkeys as symbols of devotion in Hanuman.
- Celtic mythology teems with animal guardians: the stag as sovereignty, the boar as courage, the raven as prophecy, the salmon as wisdom.
- Shamanic traditions across the world recognize spirit animals or power animals, not as fantasy, but as living allies who walk beside us in dream and waking.

To honor animals is to honor the reflection of our own spirit, our instincts, our strength, our gentleness, our freedom.

Science Confirms the Wisdom

Modern research reveals what our ancestors always knew: our survival and well-being are woven into the lives of animals.

- **Biodiversity & Balance:** Bees pollinate the crops that feed billions. Wolves balance deer populations, allowing forests to thrive. When one species disappears, the whole web trembles.
- **Health Benefits of Animals:** Connection with animals lowers blood pressure, eases anxiety, and lengthens life. Petting a dog releases oxytocin, the hormone of trust and bonding.
- **Emotional Healing:** Therapy animals comfort children with trauma, veterans with PTSD, and elders with loneliness. Their presence restores dignity and peace.
- **Empathy & Biology:** Our mirror neurons fire when we see an animal in joy or pain, proof that kinship is not only spiritual, but biological.

When we protect animals, we protect ourselves. When we dishonor them, we dishonor the very web that sustains us.

Spiritual Practice, Meeting Your Animal Ally

- Sit quietly in meditation.
- Close your eyes and breathe deeply.
- Ask inwardly: *"Which animal walks beside me?"*
- Wait patiently for an image, sound, or memory to arise. Perhaps it is the wings of an eagle, the steady gaze of a wolf, the grace of a deer, or the resilience of a turtle.
- When an animal comes to mind, breathe with it. Imagine stepping into its body. Feel its strength, its vision, its rhythm.
- Whisper: *"I honor you, kin of spirit. Teach me how to walk in balance."*
- This practice reminds us that animals are not only out there in the wild, they live within us, guiding us as inner teachers.

Practical Actions

- Support wildlife conservation efforts and habitat restoration.
- Refuse products that exploit or endanger animals.
- Reduce or shift your diet to lessen suffering and lighten Earth's burden.
- Spend time with animals, wild or domestic, not as possessions but as companions and teachers.
- Teach children reverence instead of dominance, wonder instead of fear.
- Every action toward kindness ripples through the web of life.

Keeper's Reflection – The Kinship of Eyes

There was a moment when I first looked into the eyes of an animal and truly saw. Not with the gaze of ownership or curiosity, but with recognition, the deep, startling recognition of family. In that quiet meeting, I realized: this being is not other. This being is kin.

When I look into the eyes of a wolf, I see the untamed wildness that still beats within my chest, the part of me that refuses to be caged, that runs with the wind and howls beneath the moon. When I meet the steady gaze of a horse, I feel my own strength reflected back, power not meant for conquest, but for carrying burdens with grace and endurance.

When I watch a bird rise into the endless sky, my heart remembers its longing for freedom, to move without walls, to soar beyond limits, to trust invisible currents. And when I encounter the playful joy of a dolphin dancing in waves, I feel laughter stir within me, the reminder that life was never meant to be endured only with solemnity, but celebrated with delight.

Each creature carries a piece of my own spirit, a mirror of qualities I too possess but sometimes forget. They are not ornaments to nature, nor background to human drama. They are teachers, guardians, companions on this journey of being alive.

And so I know: when I protect them, I protect myself. When I preserve their wild places, I preserve the wildness within me. When I free them from cages or suffering, I too am freed from the invisible chains around my own spirit. For life was never meant to be lived in domination, in hierarchy, in separation. It was always meant to be lived in kinship, a circle, not a ladder.

To honor animals is to remember the truth we have long forgotten: that our souls are bound together, thread by thread, howl by howl, wingbeat by wingbeat. Spirit is not free until all beings are free.

So I bow to the wolf, to the bird, to the horse, to the dolphin, and to every creature who walks, flies, swims, or crawls. I honor them as my family. And in their eyes, I remember myself.

Stories of Kinship - The Wolf's Return

For seventy years, the howl of the wolf was absent from Yellowstone. Once hunted to near extinction, the wolves had been removed in the name of safety and progress. But without them, the land forgot its rhythm. Elk multiplied without restraint, grazing tender shoots before they could grow into trees. Riverbanks eroded as willows and aspens failed to take root. Birds that nested in those trees vanished. Beavers, without wood to build their dams, disappeared. The rivers, once vibrant arteries of life, ran differently, faster, harsher, stripped of their sheltering groves.

It seemed a small thing: the absence of a predator. Yet the silence of the wolf echoed across the entire park. The balance unraveled.

Decades later, the wolves were returned. A handful of packs, small and cautious, were released back into the valleys where their ancestors once roamed. At first, the land held its breath. The elk grew wary again, moving with respect instead of domination. Willows sprouted along the water's edge. Aspens lifted their slender bodies toward the sky. Beavers returned, their dams creating ponds that nurtured fish, frogs, and waterfowl. The soil held firm, rivers curved gently again, and the pulse of life quickened.

What astonished the scientists was not simply that the ecosystem healed, but how swiftly it responded. With the return of the wolf, the land seemed to remember its song. Within years, Yellowstone grew greener, richer, more alive than it had been for generations.

The Deeper Teaching

The wolf did not restore Yellowstone by force. It restored balance by being itself, by living its role with integrity. It hunted, and in hunting, it gave life to rivers and trees, birds and fish. The wolf reminded the land of its wholeness.

And so it is with us. One life, when lived in alignment, can shift the course of rivers. One person who remembers their place in the web can heal what feels broken beyond repair. You need not carry the whole world on your shoulders. You only need to live your true role, fully, faithfully, fiercely.

The return of the wolf is not only a story of ecology. It is a story of spirit. It whispers that even after long absence, renewal is possible. Even after silence, the song can return. Even after destruction, the Earth remembers how to heal.

Reflection

When you feel too small to matter, remember the wolf. When you feel the world is too broken to mend, remember Yellowstone. Life needs every thread of the web. And sometimes, the return of just one forgotten voice can change everything.

The wolf teaches:

- Balance is restored not by domination, but by right relationship.
- Healing is possible, even after long absence.

The Earth holds memory, waiting for us to remember too.

The Child and the Bird

A young girl lost her father. With his passing, the light in her eyes dimmed, and the laughter that once bubbled from her lips grew silent. She sat often in stillness, her small hands folded in her lap, her gaze fixed not on the horizon but on the weight within her chest. The world seemed muted, its colors dulled, its songs forgotten.

One afternoon, as she sat beneath the shadow of an old oak tree, a bird descended from the sky and perched upon a nearby branch. Its feathers shimmered in the sunlight, carrying hints of gold and sky-blue, as though the heavens themselves had clothed it in memory. For a moment, the child barely noticed, grief had closed her ears, narrowed her sight.

Then the bird began to sing.

Its song was not loud, not insistent, but clear and unwavering. A thread of sound that carried through the air like a ribbon of light. The notes rose and fell, weaving joy and sorrow into a single melody. It was as though the bird knew her pain, yet sang not to erase it, but to remind her that beneath sorrow, life still breathed.

Something stirred in her heart. At first, it was only a crack in the wall of grief. But through that crack, warmth entered. For the first time in months, her lips curved into a smile. Tears flowed too, but they were different tears, tears that washed rather than weighed.

Later, when asked what had changed, she said softly, *"The bird carried me back to joy."*

The Deeper Teaching

The bird did not speak in human words, nor did it offer answers to her loss. What it gave was presence, unashamed and unbroken. Its song was both fragile and eternal. And in its singing, it awakened something she had forgotten: that joy is not the denial of grief, but its companion. That sorrow and song can live in the same heart, and together they create wholeness.

This is the way of nature. The rivers flow even after the storm. Flowers bloom again after winter's frost. The sun rises though night may feel endless. The bird taught her what sages have whispered across time: that life is not about escaping pain, but about remembering the rhythm that carries us through it.

Mystical Reflection

In many traditions, birds are messengers, bridges between earth and sky. They remind us of the soul's freedom, its capacity to rise even when burdened. To the grieving child, the bird was not only a creature; it was a spirit guide, but a thread of her father's love also woven back into her world. Its song was a reminder that nothing truly dies; it transforms, it sings in another form.

Perhaps it was her father's spirit that stirred the bird to sing. Perhaps it was the Earth herself sending comfort. Perhaps both are true. For when the natural world speaks, it speaks with many voices, birdsong, wind, water, fire, all carrying the same truth: you are not alone, and joy can return.

Lesson for Us All

When grief weighs heavy, we may look for grand gestures, for miracles to lift us. Yet often, healing arrives on small wings, in unnoticed moments: the laugh of a child, the whisper of leaves, the song of a bird at dawn. If we learn to listen, these voices guide us back to ourselves.

The child's smile was not only hers, it was a prayer answered by life itself. And so the story teaches: joy is not lost forever. It waits, quiet but constant, ready to return when we open our hearts.

Journaling Prompts

- Which animals have been most significant in my life? What did they teach me?
- How might I live differently if I saw every animal as kin, not resource?
- If I had an animal guide walking beside me today, which would it be and why?
- How can I honor the animals in my care, or those in my environment, more deeply?

A Ritual of Honoring

- Place a feather, shell, bone, or image of an animal on your altar.
- Whisper: *"I honor you, relative of spirit."*
- Offer gratitude, a song, a prayer, a gift of food or water left in nature.
- Each time you see that animal in life or dream, remember your vow of kinship.

Poetic Closing

Eyes that see me, clear as mirrors of the soul, remind me that I am never alone. Wings that lift me, carrying prayers higher than words, teach me how to rise when I forget my own strength.

Paws that walk beside me, steady and sure upon the Earth, show me how to live in balance, how to walk gently, how to belong to the ground that holds us all.

Brother, sister, teacher, friend, in feather, in fur, in scale, in skin, you are the many faces of the same spirit. Your freedom reminds me of my own. Your voice, whether roar or song, weaves into the great chorus of creation.

I honor your freedom. I honor your spirit. I honor the ancient bond that ties us, not as master and subject, but as kin in one great family.

For we are one life, beating with one pulse. We are one circle, endless and unbroken. We are one song, rising from the same breath of creation, sung through countless forms, yet always the same melody.

Keeper, remember this: To love the animal is to love yourself. To protect the wild is to protect your own heart. To walk with them in reverence is to walk in truth. For the Earth sings through all her children, and you are but one note in her eternal harmony.

8. JOIN CIRCLES OF ACTION, FIND YOUR BELONGING

The Wisdom of the Circle

From the dawn of time, humanity has gathered in circles. Around fires at night, where stories became our first teachers. In lodges, where decisions were made for the well-being of the whole tribe. Beneath the stars, where songs, dances, and rituals lifted voices into the vastness of creation. The circle is the oldest sanctuary we know.

In a circle, there is no hierarchy of corners. No one is above, no one is below. Each person faces the other, held by the same invisible center. Every voice matters, every hand contributes, every heart is seen. The circle reminds us that belonging is not given by rank but by presence.

The Earth herself moves in circles. The moon waxes and wanes in her eternal orbit. The seasons turn through their wheel of birth, growth, harvest, and rest. Planets spiral around the sun, galaxies turn in endless rotation. Even the atoms in our cells spin in circular dance. To gather in a circle is to remember what the universe has always known, that life is not linear but cyclical, sustained through connection and return.

Cultures across time and continents reveal the power of circles:

- **Indigenous Councils (Americas):** Elders, leaders, and families sat in circles to make decisions. Speaking sticks were passed so each voice could be heard, ensuring harmony with the people and with the land.
- **Celtic Stone Circles (Europe):** Places like Stonehenge aligned with solstices and equinoxes, gathering people into unity with cosmic cycles.
- **Sufi Whirling Circles (Middle East):** The dervishes whirl in circular rhythm, embodying unity with the divine heartbeat.

- **Christian Monastic Circles (Europe):** Monks prayed, chanted, and shared meals in circular formation, practicing equality before God.
- **African Drum Circles:** Rhythm bound communities together, body, spirit, and land pulsing in one heartbeat.
- **Buddhist Sangha (Asia):** Monks and lay practitioners sat in circles of meditation, embodying the truth that awakening is collective, never solitary.

The circle is humanity's oldest technology of belonging. It is how we heal, how we remember, how we act.

Science Confirms the Wisdom

Modern research now echoes what the ancients lived:

- **Group Resonance:** Studies show people's heartbeats, breath, and even brainwaves synchronize when they chant, sing, drum, or meditate together. In circle, our very biology aligns.
- **Community Health:** Loneliness is now seen as a major health risk. People in circles, whether family meals, community groups, or prayer circles, live longer, healthier, and happier lives.
- **Collective Action:** Ecological studies reveal that communities who organize in groups are far more successful in protecting watersheds, forests, and ecosystems than individuals acting alone.
- **Shared Identity:** Psychologists confirm that humans thrive when they feel part of something larger. Circles create that identity, giving strength and purpose beyond the self.

Science and spirit now sing the same song: circles heal, circles empower, circles sustain.

Spiritual Practice, Entering the Circle

Try this simple yet profound practice:

- Gather with friends, family, or neighbors. Sit in a circle.
- Place something symbolic, a candle, stone, or bowl of water, at the center. This becomes the Earth's seat in your circle.
- Take turns speaking a prayer, a gratitude, or an intention. Allow silence to rest between words.
- Sit quietly together, letting your breathing fall into rhythm. Feel the invisible thread binding you all to the same center.
- Whisper inwardly: *"The circle is unbroken. I belong. We belong."*
- Even one circle, held with sincerity, can shift the energy of a family, a community, or a nation.

Practical Actions

- **Local Circles:** Start or join a gardening group, a storytelling night, a meditation circle, or a conservation project.
- **Community Service:** Organize cleanups, food drives, or tree plantings. Every act becomes more powerful in shared hands.
- **Advocacy & Activism:** Join groups working to protect Earth's waters, forests, animals, and climate. A circle amplifies your voice.
- **Family Rituals:** Share weekly dinners, create family councils, or sit in a circle to share stories of gratitude.
- **Global Circles:** Participate in online meditations, global prayer vigils, or activist movements that weave voices from across the planet.

Every circle, small or vast, mirrors the eternal one.

Keeper's Reflection

When I sit in the circle, I remember who I am. When I act in the circle, I remember what we can do. Alone, I may falter. Together, we rise. The Earth herself is circle, the horizon round, the womb round, the seasons turning in eternal return.

When I honor the circle, I step back into the truth that life is shared. My belonging is not earned, it is given by the simple fact of being part of Earth's great community. And when we gather in circle, we remember that the fire still burns, the song is still sung, and the circle is unbroken.

Stories of Circles - The Circle of Coals

Long ago, when choices had to be made, the people did not hide behind walls or sit in rows, one above another. There were no thrones, no stages, no barriers of power. Instead, they came together in a circle around glowing coals, the fire alive at the center. Its light reached every face equally, casting no shadows of hierarchy. In its warmth, all were reminded: the fire belonged to everyone, and so did the future.

The council always began with silence. Not silence of emptiness, but silence of listening, to the fire, to the wind moving beyond the lodge, to the beating of their own hearts. Only then did the voices rise, one by one, like sparks rising into night.

The eldest spoke first, drawing wisdom from memory as one draws water from a deep well. They carried the stories of those who had walked before, ensuring the past was not forgotten. Their words reminded the people of what had been endured, and what had already been overcome.

Then the mothers spoke, their voices woven with the rhythm of nurture. They asked, *"What will feed the children? What will keep them safe? What will teach them to grow with kindness?"* Their words were not only for their own offspring, but for the generations yet unborn.

The hunters and gatherers added their voices, speaking of the needs of the journey, of the herds and the rivers, of the strength required for survival. Their concerns carried the urgency of the present, food, shelter, protection.

But the circle did not end there. For after wisdom and nurture, after provision and strength, came the children. They were not dismissed as too young to understand, nor silenced by the weight of age. Instead, they were invited to listen, to ask, to learn, and finally, to retell.

No decision was complete until the youngest among them could repeat it back in their own simple words. This was the test of the circle: that the future could carry the choice as clearly as the past. Only then did the people know their decision was whole. For if a child could understand, the path was safe enough to guide the steps of them all.

The fire itself was the teacher. Its circle never broke. Its light warmed all equally. Its coals glowed brightest when tended together. *"This,"* the elders would say, *"is the way of the fire: it teaches us that decisions made in circle belong to everyone, and the warmth of wisdom must be shared."*

And so the circle of coals became more than a council, it became a way of life. It reminded the people that power lies not in the loudest voice, but in the shared rhythm of many hearts. It taught them that no future can be strong unless even the youngest can walk upon it with clarity.

Even today, the story lingers. When we gather in circles of action, of family, of community, we echo those ancient coals. We remember that the light must touch every face, the silence must precede every word, and the decision is not complete until the smallest among us can understand.

For the circle of coals is not only a memory of the past, it is a living pattern, inviting us again and again to choose together, to listen deeply, and to walk forward as one.

The Community Garden

In a neighborhood where boarded windows outnumbered blooming trees, where the silence of abandonment weighed heavier than the hum of life, a few neighbors looked around and said, *"We cannot wait any longer. If life is to return, it must begin with us."*

On a forgotten lot choked with weeds, litter, and broken bottles, they began. One patch at a time. One stone pulled, one root dug out, one stubborn thorn bush cut away. The ground was hard, compacted by years of neglect, but so were they. The first day yielded little more than sore backs and blistered hands. But they kept coming back, carrying borrowed shovels, buckets of water, and packets of seeds shared among them like sacred offerings.

And slowly, the barren soil began to soften.

The first shoots were small, almost fragile, green threads breaking through cracked earth. Tomatoes, beans, corn, squash. At first, the neighbors thought they were planting food. But soon they realized they were planting something far greater.

Children who once played in cracked streets found themselves chasing butterflies between rows of sunflowers that rose like golden guardians of hope. Elders, who had thought their wisdom forgotten, sat at the edges of the rows, teaching little hands how to loosen soil gently, how to pull a carrot without breaking its stem, how to listen for the stories the earth was always whispering.

Strangers became neighbors. Neighbors became friends. And friends became family.

The garden was not only harvest, it was medicine. It healed loneliness with laughter. It replaced hunger with nourishment. It softened despair with the fragrance of basil, the sweetness of strawberries, the crunch of cucumbers pulled fresh from the vine.

On Saturdays, when the sun was high and the week's labors complete, they gathered for meals made from their own hands' work. Under a makeshift trellis woven with morning glories, they shared soups and stews, roasted corn and fresh bread. Music sometimes rose spontaneously, a guitar strummed, a drumbeat on a bucket, voices weaving into song. It was as if the garden itself was singing through them, a hymn of renewal echoing from the soil.

One man, his palms still dark with soil, spoke words that lingered in every heart: *"We didn't just plant seeds in the ground. We planted ourselves back into the circle of life. "*

The garden became their sanctuary. Children learned the names of plants as if they were old friends. Elders saw their wisdom carried forward in new generations. Those who once felt invisible found themselves seen, needed, valued.

And in that space, something mystical unfolded: the garden became more than food, more than medicine. It became a mirror of possibility. It reminded everyone that even in the hardest places, life insists on returning. Flowers bloom through cracks in concrete. Hope rises where despair once lived. Connection grows when people dare to plant together.

Years later, when vines curled around sturdy trellises and fruit hung heavy from branches, people came from outside the neighborhood to see what had been created. They expected vegetables. What they found was community. They found people laughing, children running, elders teaching, and music rising into the sky.

And always, in the center of it all, the soil, dark, living, forgiving, holding the roots not only of plants, but of people who had remembered what it means to belong.

The Community Garden was never only about vegetables. It was about remembering that humanity itself grows best in circles of care. It was about rediscovering the sacred truth that when we sow connection, compassion, and hope, we reap abundance that no market can measure.

It stood as a testament: even in forgotten places, even in neglected soil, life can return, if we have the courage to plant it.

Journaling Prompts

- When have I felt most supported by a group or circle?
- What circle in my life do I most long to join or create?
- How might I invite others into sacred community with me?
- What does *"belonging"* mean in my spiritual and daily life?

A Ritual of Circle-Building

- Invite friends or family into a circle.
- Place objects in the center: a stone, a bowl of water, a candle, a feather.
- Go around the circle. Each person offers one word of blessing.
- End with joined hands or shared silence.

The circle does not end when you stand, it continues in every step you take together.

Poetic Closing

Circle of fire, that warms the spirit, that burns away fear, that lights the way through the darkness.

Circle of stone, that anchors the ground, that holds memory older than time, that teaches us endurance and patience.

Circle of breath, that moves through every being, that rises and falls with the tides, that connects us to the forests, the oceans, the skies.

Circle of bone, that shapes our bodies, that reminds us we are Earth in form, that carries the lineage of all who came before.

Circles within circles, woven through seasons, spiraling through generations, turning with moon and sun, with heartbeat and drumbeat, with prayer and silence.

Unbroken, eternal, woven not of power or possession, but of presence and love. The circle does not judge, it does not exclude, it does not end. It calls all who are willing to sit in reverence, to listen with humility, to rise with devotion.

Keeper, step in. Feel the warmth of the fire on your skin, the strength of the stone at your back, the rhythm of breath in your chest, the memory of bone in your being. Know that you belong. Know that you are seen. Know that you are part of the song that never ceases, the prayer that never ends.

Step into the circle, the home that was waiting for you before you were born, the home that will carry you long after you return to the Earth.

Step in, not as guest, but as family. Not as stranger, but as Keeper. The circle is here. The circle is whole. The circle is home.

EPILOGUE, THE KEEPER'S DAWN

The journey you have walked through these pages is not an ending. It is a beginning.

You have listened to the call of the Earth. You have awakened to the great web of life, sat in silence with the stones, followed the song of waters, listened to the counsel of trees, and felt the heartbeat of Gaia echoing through your chest. You have entered the Circle of Keepers, spoken your vow, and embraced the shifting frequencies of now. You have glimpsed the path ahead, not as a dream, but as a living invitation.

You have been given practices to shape your days, rituals of prayer, reflection, and devotion. You have received the Keeper's Action Guide, offering ways to heal soil, water, trees, animals, and community. These are not just tasks. They are living prayers, bridges of reciprocity that bind your life to Earth's renewal.

And now, beloved Keeper, you stand at dawn.

The Threshold of Becoming

There is no greater illusion than separation. You are not apart from the Earth. You are Earth herself, breathing, walking, remembering through human form.

To walk as a Keeper is to awaken each day to this truth. It is to see your body as soil, water, fire, and air. It is to know that when you love the Earth, you love yourself; and when you harm her, you wound yourself.

This path does not ask for perfection. It does not demand that you fix the whole world. It asks for something far more powerful and far more possible: that you live with remembrance. That you live with reverence. That you live each step as prayer:

- When you touch soil, touch it as the body of the Mother.

- When you drink water, drink it as blessing.
- When you walk, let each step fall gently as an offering.
- When you breathe, know the trees breathe with you.
- When you speak, let kindness be the seed of every word.
- When you act, let love be your compass.

These are not small things. These are the great things. This is how worlds are changed, not only by grand gestures, but by steady choices, repeated each day, that ripple outward and shape the future.

The Circle Extends

You are not alone. Even when silence surrounds you, the Circle of Keepers is near, an unbroken ring that stretches far beyond what the eyes can see.

Around you stand the ancestors, their memory alive in your bones. Behind you are the elders, carrying wisdom hard-earned. Before you are the children, carrying promise like seeds. Beside you are animals who teach balance, rivers who sing of flow, stones who whisper of endurance, forests who breathe renewal, and stars who remind you of eternity. All are Keepers, each one holding their place in the circle, each one tending the eternal flame of life.

Every act of devotion adds to this fire. A kind word spoken, a seed planted, a prayer whispered at dawn, all are sparks. Each strengthens the web that connects all beings, weaving threads between those who came before and those yet to be born.

When you walk this path, you do not walk alone. You are the dream of your ancestors made flesh. You are the guardian of the present moment. And you are already the ancestor of the future, shaping with every breath the world your children's children will inherit.

Remember: the circle does not break. It widens. It carries you, shelters you, and calls you into your place. To forget this truth is to feel adrift. To remember it is to stand unshaken.

The circle is unbroken. And you are part of its fire.

A Call to Action

The Earth is rising. Her heartbeat quickens, her frequencies shift, her song grows louder. She is calling, not faintly, but with power. You hear it in the thunder of rivers, the cry of birds, the winds that shake the trees, and the chambers of your own heart.

The time for forgetting is over. The time for remembering is now. The time for apathy is over. The time for devotion is now. The time for despair is over. The time for courage is now.

You are not powerless. You are powerful, not by domination or control, but by connection. Not by force, but by the quiet, radiant strength of love. Every choice you make, every word you speak, every seed you plant, every kindness you extend, these ripple outward, unseen but unstoppable, weaving new patterns into the web of life:

- Do not underestimate the small acts:
- A whispered prayer over water.
- A smile offered to a stranger.
- A tree planted in bare ground.
- A child taught to listen to the wind.

These are not small things. These are the foundations of a new world.

This is the Keeper's dawn, a threshold where past and future meet in your hands. You are both the ancestor of tomorrow and the guardian of today. Stand where you are. Rise with the Earth. And remember:

The circle is unbroken. The fire is alive. The call is clear. And the time is now.

A Keeper's Blessing

- Keeper of Earth, child of soil, child of water, child of fire, child of air.
- You are breath of the Mother, light of the Father, dream of the ancestors, hope of the descendants.
- Walk gently. Walk bravely. Walk with love.
- The Earth walks with you. The circle holds you. The fire burns within you. The path is endless, and it begins with you.

www.ingramcontent.com/pod-product-compliance
Lightning Source LLC
LaVergne TN
LVHW020716110826
845149LV00012B/2294

* 9 7 9 8 9 9 3 1 3 8 5 6 5 *